JESUS
APPROACHES

Other Books by Elizabeth M. Kelly

The Rosary: A Path into Prayer

*May Crowning, Mass, and Merton and Other Reasons
I Love Being Catholic*

2013: A Book of Grace-Filled Days

2014: A Book of Grace-Filled Days

Heaven in You & You in Heaven

JESUS
APPROACHES

What Contemporary Women Can Learn about Healing,
Freedom & Joy from the Women of the New Testament

ELIZABETH M. KELLY

LOYOLA PRESS.
A JESUIT MINISTRY
Chicago

LOYOLA PRESS.
A JESUIT MINISTRY

www.loyolapress.com

Cover art credit: The Visitation, 1528–30 fresco by Pontormo, Jacopo (1494–1557); San Michele, Carmignano, Prato, Italy

ISBN: 978-0-8294-4472-8
Library of Congress Control Number: 2017942124

Printed in the United States of America.
21 22 23 24 25 26 27 28 29 30 Versa 10 9 8 7 6 5 4 3

CONTENTS

For my mother, Mary,
for your fidelity to prayer and
adoration of the Blessed Sacrament

OPENING: EPISTLE

"For it is the Christian community which 'holds' the risen Lord in its depths and retells the story of his life."
—John Wickham, SJ

Dear Sister,

The first thing I do is this: I come to the water. This is where I hear the Lord best. This is where I sense him most, in the wind and the steadiness of the waves against the shore, in that restful depth of sight that stretches out to the horizon. Here I can breathe him in as air.

I have always been attracted to large bodies of water this way. As it happens, the retreat I have selected this time on a large lake is one my father visited on many occasions as a younger man, when he would come yearly to pray and to rest in the Lord. It is a comfort to me that he walked along these same paths and prayed in this chapel and took in this view. I imagine him here with his father's heart, praying and longing and hoping at this shore—even for the very *me* he had no idea I would later become. And I long for the Lord, as did my father before me. The constancy of this is a happy birthright, the inheritance of a holy yearning: the desire to steal oneself away to be with Jesus.

I come to the water at nightfall. And I make my way down to the shore, down the steps, down the path, over the rocks—descending—and, after settling in, I listen for the evening waves lapping against the rocks and watch the sun set as the world falls into sleepy, summer darkness. A storm brews in the distance. Lightning flashes far off in the east, and I think of you, Lord. I sense you, Jesus, stirring under the waters. How I long to see you, long for you to rise from the darkness, to gather yourself into human flesh and bone and walk on the water and call to me just as you did to your friends so long ago, "Take heart, it is I. Do not be afraid." Would you come to me on the water, Lord? Would you rise and come and spread your unfailing arms and call me to you, as you did Peter: "Come"? Would I have courage enough to say yes, and with my whole heart and without reservation or hesitation would I reach for you, step out onto the glassy waves and know that you are Lord? Would I say yes to so much grace? Grace enough to make it all the way, to lay my head upon your heart and rest in your embrace? Would you hold me, Jesus, hold me up over the turbulent sea?

The next thing I do: I think of you, sister. I bring you with me to the water, to the shore. I bring you and your secret heart here, down on the rocks, and I hold you before Jesus, before the Beloved. I take your hand and smile at you and say, "Do not be afraid, take heart. It really is Jesus!" It doesn't matter that I may not know your name and that you may not know me. I know that ache you carry, the weariness that sometimes creeps into your bones, the fear, the worry, *will it be all right?* I know that deep abiding hope in Jesus that battles with a sense of exhaustion at the world—the world. You know. So much needs mending—and we are made for mending. So much needs a healing, feminine touch—and we are rebuffed, or perhaps our cupboards are bare, our coffers feel too empty. It is a constant knife to the heart—the scandal of poverty, abortion, pornography, the injustice of it all, rejection, addiction, divorce, betrayal, illness, financial collapse, to be misunderstood, to be misjudged, accused, the meanness of our bad habits and the cruelty of our disordered hearts. I know the failure of human love and the struggle to hope. *Who will mend me?* you ask. I know. My heart is broken too.

So I bring you to the water, and I hold those places in you that no one knows, that no one understands, the part of you that will go to your grave never having been visited by anyone but Jesus. This is your most secret heart, the one you take to silent adoration and pray, pray, pray that Jesus will see and love and heal. I stand here at the shore and I hold you before the Lord of this sea. The lightning flashes, and I stand in the gap on your behalf, just as my father stood here again and again, stood here for me.

We have work to do. The world needs us—it needs you, needs me, needs us to be the people we were created to be. It needs our gifts and prayers and hopes and lives of faithful, holy-woman service. More than ever the world needs you—though it may never love you. This is an era that desperately needs a faithful Christian woman, not a perfect woman, not a woman who has never failed nor fallen, but a woman who has fallen in love with the truth, a woman in love with Jesus, a woman willing to have her heart broken and paraded through the streets. Do we have the courage to fall in love that much? To be used without fear of loss or diminishment? To be humbled and honed and sent back out, wounded healers, teachers still learning, leaders not always so certain, companions in need of friendship, mothers and daughters and wives and menders who need mending? Jesus is not calling only Mary or Mother Teresa; he is calling Martha and Mary Magdalene, too. Jesus is not waiting for you to be perfect; he is waiting for you to say yes.

Yes to grace, yes to healing, yes to humbling, yes to forgiveness and mercy, yes to the Cross and Good Friday, to the chilly, silent tomb and to that warming glow of Easter-morning resurrection. Yes to death and being made new. Yes to a mission that, by all accounts, on the surface, seems sure to fail. Yes to the mystery and wonder of embodying beauty, truth, and goodness. Can't you feel it? Don't you know it, way down deep, some place ever-ancient and ever-new in the very heart of you? Jesus says, "Come."

Maybe we have been lax too long about our work in the world, or distracted by the nonessential, or afraid we are not enough, or just plain tired, and the wound that has resulted from our neglect can be healed only by our feminine attention, our womanish prayer, our female instincts, our likeness to the bride of Christ. Men have their work too, and we join them on many fronts, in the church and in the wider world, but there is work that God is giving to women that men cannot do, not in the same way. Not because men are lacking, but because men and women are different. (We needn't make more of this than it is.) But perhaps we've stayed too long at the shore, sought too long the safety of the boat. We might be tired and frightened, some of us might feel broken and so lonely, but Jesus is here, and he says, "Come." How will you answer? What will you do?

There are things the world wants you to forget, but Jesus asks us to remember, to remember who you are in Christ: *"Remember who you are in me."* Remember the lavish grace he wants to pour out upon your heart—the mercy, forgiveness, courage, and strength just within your reach. The touch of Jesus on your heart does not change only you: *it changes everything.*

Woman, rise, take heart; let's help each other reach together for the Lord. Let's walk on the glassy, uncertain sea and let Jesus meet us and heal us and teach us and hold us all the way to heaven. He will tend you, every part of you. He will tend you, strengthen and prepare you, and send you forth. Come, let us be women about our father's business.

1

MAGDALENE

"Woman, why are you weeping?"
—John 20:15

My prayer was this: Mary Magdalene, show me the Jesus you knew.

In the half darkness that is dawn, your eyes can deceive you. Objects appear in disguise. The dark figure looming ahead—is it a wild animal ready to pounce or the stump of a dead tree? Even as the planets are hurtling through the heavens at unimaginable speed, that hour—of moving from darkness to daylight—can feel too still. The world would not yet call that early morning Easter. As far as she knew, all of creation was still haunted by a confused and cruel emptiness. But this is the hour that would become, in some ways, her hour, Magdalene's hour.

How could the sun rise on such a world? The half light echoes the great, sorrowful question she carries, making it heavier, denser. She presses on to the place where they laid him, that one she loves and who loves her. He is the one who gave her hope; but it wasn't just hope—it was a new life, a radically new way to be in the world. She remembers that first day so well, weeping at his feet in joy and relief and such extraordinary surprise.

Who was this man? Could there be such forgiveness? Was it real, or had she imagined it? The days grew brighter then, and she knew peace, freshness. Those precious years of moving from place to place

1

throughout Galilee, years of witnessing so much healing. And his words, lingering so sweetly: "Woman, neither do I condemn you."

But then betrayal, accusation, torture, death.

What now, Lord? What would you have me do now?

Perhaps there will be rest at least, there will be peace for him at least, she thinks. She buries her sorrow along with the memory of his death and continues to the tomb.

Her eyes strain to see the way. The ointments and oils in her arms feel too heavy to carry, but they draw her forward to the task ahead. That's assuming she can even reach him; there's the stone to be moved. It's far too heavy for her to roll back from the entrance.

I can't think of that yet. She watches her feet stepping out in front of her, hesitant, unsure. They don't feel as if they belong to her body, walking through this darkened world. Her thoughts drift away.

Finally, she is standing at the tomb and finds that the stone has been moved away from the entrance. Maybe someone anticipated her coming. She steps into the sepulchre and sees that nothing but linens remain where Jesus rested. *How can this be? What can it mean? Where is he? Who took him? What could anyone want with disturbing his body? Will there be no end to this madness?*

She turns back, rushing to tell the others what has happened: "They have taken the Lord out of the tomb! I don't know where he is." They must see it for themselves. They race to the tomb, Peter and the others, gasping for air, for understanding. What Magdalene has said is true, and their hearts are heavy and confused. They return home—what else can they do?

But Magdalene stays. This will be her home for now, the place where she last was with him. There must be something of him left here, inside. *I will stay here awhile.* When the others have gone, she leans to look into the cave. And there sit two men dressed in white.

One asks, "Woman, why are you weeping?"

"They have taken my Lord away and I don't know where they have put him." She suddenly feels awkward, startled by their question. She turns away. It is still early and she is tired with grief. But there, another man. Where did he come from and who is he? The gardener? Perhaps he was the one who moved the body of Jesus. Perhaps he knows where Jesus is.

Her voice is weak, but she is determined. "Sir, have you taken him? Please tell me where so I may go and get him."

She could not know what was about to break upon her and the whole world. She could not yet comprehend the extraordinary privilege about to be extended to her—a woman of absolutely no import in that ancient world.

But then, he calls her by name: "Mary."

Women from Magdalene's time would collect their tears in tiny vials. I learned this in the Holy Land from a Catholic archaeologist born and raised in Jerusalem. He told me that when a woman married, she would give the vial to her husband—that is to say, she handed over to his care everything that was most precious to her, in sorrow and in joy. In the Gospels, we know Magdalene as the woman freed of seven demons, and in tradition we also know her as the adulterous woman the Pharisees wanted to stone. That same woman who anointed Jesus with oil and her tears and then dried him with her hair, who, having been forgiven much, loved much. When Magdalene washed Christ's feet, some believe it may have been with the tears from her little vial, tears that marked the most precious moments of her life. This is precisely what she was doing, giving to Jesus everything most precious to her, pouring out upon him, entrusting to him in the humblest way possible, everything that mattered to her.

This is the Magdalene I treasure most and so long to be.

Anointing Heart

Surprisingly, as you enter the Church of the Holy Sepulchre, buried deep in the heart of Jerusalem, the first thing you encounter is the anointing stone. Archaeologists believe they have located the kind of anointing stone upon which Jesus' body was prepared for the tomb. That stone was discovered in the area where Jesus and other crucified persons would have been anointed for burial. Over the centuries, as pilgrims paid homage to that traditional stone, it began to wear away, and so another stone, one that protects the archeological find, rests above it. And here is where pilgrims and popes now kneel and pray. Some rest their heads and hands upon the stone. Some place rosaries and other devotional objects on it, believing in the power of sharing the presence of something sacred, if only for a moment.

I see one young woman place her sick child on the stone. The child's limbs are bent in stiff, unnatural contortions. She wails and convulses at the momentary loss of her mother's touch, and there appears to be no instant healing. But you can see in the eyes of the mother all the longing, hope, trust, and belief she carries with her to this holy place. She is Magdalene too, giving to Jesus everything most precious to her, in joy and sorrow, trusting her deepest woman's heart to his care.

If you get close enough to it, you will discover that the stone has a distinct aroma. Some come to pour myrrh and nard over it—the traditional anointing oils—and then soak up those oils with a cloth to be taken home. Some use cloths that have the image of Christ's face on them, something akin to commemorating Veronica's veil. I have always been attracted to Veronica's story, and to Magdalene's. I think, if I could have, I would have offered some small comfort to our Lord too. We are embodied creatures, and something about this traditional devotion and the way it engages the body speaks deeply to me. If I could, I would anoint my Lord.

So this is what I did. I returned to the Holy Sepulchre early in the morning, when there are fewer tourists and visitors and pilgrims about. At that hour it is a much more quiet, gentle space for the gesture I was about to undertake. It was early morning when Magdalene visited the tomb, so it seemed an especially appropriate hour. I knelt at one of the corners of the stone and poured out the myrrh and nard I had bought the night before. As I began to wipe it with a cloth—and yes, mine bears the image of Christ's face—I prayed again the prayer of my heart: *Mary Magdalene, show me the Jesus you knew.*

Who knows how such things are received in the Heart of Heaven, but I knelt there, giving Jesus every sorrow and joy I could, pouring out the oils, and then gathering them back up with as much tenderness and affection as I could muster. These oils represented everything most precious to me: all my repentance and hope for forgiveness, all my grief. I kept thinking about how heartbroken Magdalene must have been in that moment: *Oh Jesus, if I could, I would anoint you with oil and wash you in my tears, dry you with my hair. If I could, I would give you everything most precious to me.*

Magdalene, more than most, must have understood my heart in that moment. She had anointed him more than once—in life, and in death.

I am reminded of the life Magdalene knew before that shocking and public introduction to the teacher from Nazareth. It must have held an emptiness and shame that few fully withstand—not without drinking or overeating or doing something to numb the pain. They dragged her into the temple and brought her, a known sinner, before the crowd. "Caught in adultery!" You can feel the scorching condemnation emanating from the pages of your Bible. Hypocrisy is too easy and available a sin. Few go untouched by it.

The scribes and Pharisees address Jesus: "In the law Moses commanded us to stone such women. Now what do you say?" (John 8:5).

Yes, there is the law. There are those who fall in love with the logic of the institution, the rules that govern and appoint it and give it form, the deep theological, philosophical postures of mind that build the walls and ceiling of our beloved church. There is so much there to love and to honor, but Jesus makes very plain that it is not enough to love the law. Those strong walls, that impenetrable roof—they do not exist for themselves but only to protect the tender beating heart that dwells inside them. Even the most dazzling theological brilliance, if not first formed by love, just becomes a crushing and cruel cleverness.

Nor is it enough to *love* the truth; you must *fall in love* with the truth and let it have its way with you—that is, let him have his way with you. I am convinced that if you cannot fall in love with Jesus, you will never be able to truly fall in love with anyone else.

The extraordinary beauty of Magdalene was precisely this: she was able and willing to fall in love with Jesus and with all that such loving would imply. The words that first pierced her heart may be some of the best recognized in the world—they are a command for all of us: "Let you who is without sin cast the first stone." And one by one, accusers dropped their stones and walked away. And every honest reader in the world breathes a deep sigh of relief and gratitude.

The men so ready to stone her had no heart beating inside the walls of their ideas and self-righteousness. They were empty inside, more barren than the desert, and nothing would grow there. But fragrant, beautiful blossoms exploded inside her. And when her Lord would later be taken in such cruelty and betrayal—as many were indifferently entertained at the spectacle—her heart would break inside the walls of her fledgling faith. Because she loved much.

But there, before the crowd, she wouldn't deny that that was right where she belonged—rocks of disgust and judgment ready to fly at her. It's a place not too many of us occupy, not literally. But maybe in these days, the whole church understands a bit better the heart of public scandal, failing and falling before the eyes of all. For some it may be an addiction, or a serious personal sin exposed, or the various scandals that haunt our holy priesthood. In my case, it was the one thing a "real" Catholic never does: divorce.

"Her sins, which were many, are forgiven" (Luke 7:47).

There is a reason God warns us so sternly about divorce. The human heart was not designed to be freely given away and then taken back. It is an impossible maneuver, like trying to pour the ocean into a cup. And God is not in the business of setting the human heart to impossible tasks, those that go against the true nature of our creation; that would frustrate his beloved sons and daughters. He asks much of the human heart, certainly, but never anything that is impossible without his grace. Grace perfects nature, Aquinas tells us; it does not revise it, not to save face or even to suit a miracle. And we are invited to cooperate with it. God will never force himself upon us.

You could ask almost any beloved figure of the Old or New Testament—King David or the apostle Peter—and they would tell you this is true: vows that are made cannot be unmade, only broken. And this leads to every kind of sin and misery.

Divorce was unthinkable to me. I had watched my parents approach their sixtieth wedding anniversary. I had spent so many years single that when I finally married, I thought I knew better than most the gift I was being given, and I planned to treasure and protect it with my entire being. I ended up divorced anyway.

My friends would say things like, "It didn't really take. You were never *really* married, even the church would say so." It's true; years later, the church did say so sacramentally; we lived in the same house for less than a year and there were very serious problems from the start, but that wasn't the point. Sacrament or no, my heart was broken. I'd lost my whole world, a world I truly believed in and had given myself over to completely.

The man I married has led a generous life of service and helped many people. He must be in good favor with heaven, and yet, there we were, having made such an excruciating decision before God and our friends. For us, for our families and community, the heartbreak was intense and public. I had a whole new understanding of the public aspect of the Crucifixion. It is one thing to suffer in the shadows of your darkened room; it is quite another to have your broken heart paraded through the streets.

But marriage is a public sacrament, a reality based in community; maybe it's fitting that divorce should be too. Whatever the case, I had a growing sense that Magdalene wanted to teach me something about it.

"She has done what she could" (Mark 14:8).

Magdalene and I were first properly introduced in Rome, and more specifically, in the Redemptoris Mater Chapel inside the Apostolic Palace. The mosaics inside were commissioned in honor of Pope St. John Paul II's fiftieth anniversary of his ordination to the priesthood, and it is this chapel that is reserved for exclusive use by the pope. I was invited to a tour quite by accident when I was living in Rome, and I had no idea what I was about to experience.

Entering Vatican City is always a rather memorable event. As you pass the Swiss Guards in their colorful regalia, you know that you are in the presence of something noble, something to be protected with strength and even violence if necessary. But crossing the threshold of the chapel was literally breathtaking. I gasped and began to cry silently. I couldn't explain my reaction. Was I sensing the holiness that lingered after the many masses celebrated there? Or was what still hung in the air the prayers of the artists who created the sweeping mosaics covering the walls and ceiling? I couldn't tell you. I stumbled into a pew, my mouth still agape, eyes wide and weeping. Our guide was incredibly wise and told us to spend an hour in prayer with the mosaics before she would give us an introduction to the chapel and its history.

I took a quick survey of every surface and the salvation story each recounted. Jonah and the fish, Noah's ark, Moses parting the Red Sea on one wall. On another, the Crucifixion, Pentecost, the Annunciation, Jesus washing the feet of his disciples, and of course, the mother of the Redeemer surrounded by a communion of saints. But it was the back left corner that caught my attention. I was taken with one particular image: Christ receiving the tears and anointing of a woman. The Gospel says the woman was "a known sinner" (in Luke 7:36–50). Tradition tells us it might be Magdalene. Over the centuries and especially during the Middle Ages, Magdalene became a kind of composite of the troubled women Jesus saved. The artist in this case may have meant to represent the anonymous penitent of Luke's Gospel who anointed Jesus' feet—her face is mostly hidden and bears no identifiable characteristics, adding to her portrayal as the "penitent everyman"—but I immediately identify her as Magdalene.

With a broken alabaster jar nearby, she is as you might picture her: covered in a gray tunic, kneeling, bent and low before Jesus. She carefully cradles one of his feet in her hands—almost as if she were anticipating the wound it will soon carry for her. She is drying the foot with her hair. You sense she is about to lower herself further still and kiss the foot. There is more than surrender and gratitude in her posture; her expression is almost an anticipation of the suffering and sorrow ahead, the joy of the rising that will follow, and her tears are pouring out upon and entering into, comingling with, all these precious mysteries. She knows this is possible not by her effort or repentance but by his forgiveness, his perfect love.

In fact, everything about her—her posture, her comportment, the drape of her hair and caress of her hands—leads in only one direction: to Christ. A Christ who *receives*.

Yes, he loved first, offered forgiveness and grace first, but in this moment he receives, and he receives from a woman her loving touch. The radical significance of this act in a culture in which women were thought of by most as possessions, at times ritually unclean, or even slaves, cannot be overemphasized.

He lowers himself too, to meet her, reaching out to receive her. His eyes look gently upon her and her humble gesture. As she offers him her lowliness and repentance and affection, he is already beginning to raise her up out of the dirt. He is dressed in a strikingly red garment. Even with years of studying painting and art history, my eyes have never seen this red before. The contrast of Magdalene's washed-out gray attire and the vibrancy of the blood-red robe of Christ is more shocking than any photo can capture. It must speak to the new life that the blood of Christ can bring to anyone—no matter how lifeless that person has become in any manner of sin—if he or she is willing to become lowly and vulnerable.

The great lesson depicted here is Magdalene's awareness. Unlike the Pharisees seated at the table, she knows what it means to be in the presence of Jesus, and all her attention and affection are directed in repentance and gratitude toward him. But the even greater lesson is the knowledge that Christ receives her tenderly, generously—and draws near. I understand in a new way that this is how Jesus asks us to receive him and his good gifts—especially those that arrive wrapped up as other people. I pray for the capacity to receive greatly, earnestly, all the love and forgiveness and grace that is offered—all that is so very much needed—and to draw near to him, arms and heart and soul wide open.

I bought a book with an image of that mosaic in it, and I carry the image with me when I travel. I have it in my office and my prayer room. Years later, I go back to that mosaic, that anointing moment, when I meditate on the "sinful woman" in Luke 7 while completing the Ignatian Spiritual Exercises. Typically, when you are moving through the Exercises, you want to concentrate on what Jesus is doing and dwell with him, in this case his telling of the story of the creditor and the two debtors, the creditor canceling both debts, great and small. Jesus questions: "Which of them will love more?" Then he sends the woman forth forgiven: "Your faith has saved you; go in peace."

But in this one instance, in my imagination, I leave the presence of Jesus and follow Magdalene home after she receives Jesus' blessing. Just this once I abandon form and I stay instead with Magdalene—but this is a new Magdalene, one radically altered by the redeeming love of Christ.

Her step is light, anonymous. She moves through the crowd, no longer of any particular notice. Those who knew her before her encounter with Christ see that something has changed; everything has changed, though they cannot quite name it. She is quiet and goes about her work with humility and a still heart. Her eyes are clear and her comportment upright. The scurrilous glances of others seem no longer to penetrate. Instead they are met with a holy, quiet, untouchable joy. It is disarming.

As I watch her move through her new world, I see that, in a place that no one but Jesus can touch, she knows the reality of a living forgiveness that has washed away all of the sin and death she carried. Her need has been great, but the Giver of good gifts has been—is—far greater. She has done what she could and for this, she has been received in heaven's fullness. Her love grows.

"I have seen the Lord!"

We present-day pilgrims will spend our last day in Galilee on the Mount of Beatitudes. The sky is huge and empty and blue, the sun warm, the breeze lovely. Under the thick cover of ancient trees, several outdoor altars have been erected to accommodate the numerous pilgrims who travel here to celebrate Mass together. Our small group is fortunate to be given a private little corner with a sweeping view of the Sea of Galilee just before the noonday siesta. Soon the grounds will become virtually empty, and we will remain to pray, first a long prayer of forgiveness and then the Mass in which our priest will emphasize healing. It is an especially generous apex to our pilgrimage.

The Beatitudes are carved in Latin (taken from the Vulgate) and scattered throughout the grounds. Our altar is engraved with Matthew 5:5: "Blessed are those who mourn, for they shall be comforted." The words wash over me. I have been in mourning a long while, and I know well that it can be difficult to know when to let go of something that has no real resolution. At what point is it okay to move on? I'm thinking of this when we begin the forgiveness prayer. I ask God to expand the capacity I have to receive whatever he wishes to give: comfort, conviction, instruction, anything. *Beati qui lugent . . .*

As the priest begins leading us through a thorough reflection on the people and pains that might need forgiving, including ourselves, the Spirit moves. I hear it in the voices of others as they pray; I see it in their tears and feel it in my own. There's much that needs forgiveness and forgiving in me, and I collapse into the mercy of Jesus there under the ancient trees that shade the very earth where his public ministry of healing and teaching and saving the lost began.

One thing age teaches you—if you're willing to learn it—is that being judgmental is exhausting. "Judge not" is not simply a command to protect others but also a law designed with the intention of protecting you—"lest you be judged." I have grown so weary of the false ways my self-righteousness, even toward myself, have buried me in grief. I am so ready to be done with it, to give it to Jesus, to leave it at the foot of the Cross where he paid the debt in full for my critical heart. The prayer time for forgiveness is filled with my tears, and I'm grateful for the ability to weep; sometimes weeping is absolutely the right thing. It is somehow even more fitting in this location with this geography. If I could, I would weep myself a little stream of water that trickled down from my eyes and onto the soil and down the mountain and into the sea—that sea he calmed, that sea he walked upon—and my tears would find him in that beautiful body of water. They would glisten in the sun and dance beneath his feet as he walked out toward the frightened apostles. If I could.

Soon it is my turn for private prayer. When the priest stands before me, his first words cannot be a coincidence. "Remember the words of the Lord to Magdalene," he says, and my heart catches. "'Do not hold on to me, for I have not yet ascended to my father. Go and tell the others and I will see you in Galilee.'" I can hardly take the words in. "You're clinging to the foot of the Cross," he continues, "but Jesus doesn't want you to cling to it any longer."

Then the priest gives me very simple instructions: I am to imagine holding in my hands all that has troubled and broken my heart, and then lift it up, give it up to the Lord. I'm not supposed to lower my arms until I have given it all to him. And that is that; the priest moves on to the next person.

So, there I stand, at the Sea of Galilee, on the Mount of Beatitudes, the words "mourn" and "comforted" ringing in my ears, tears streaming down my face, my hands raised above my head holding up my grief and loss and sense of being so misunderstood before God. And it is as if Jesus himself suddenly appears before me in dazzling white robes and smiles and says, "Woman, why are you weeping? Whom are you looking for?"

It can be the hardest thing when intuitively it should be the easiest—to let go of the pain, to truly and completely entrust it to Jesus, to place it at the foot of the Cross, and never pick it up again. Our pain is precious to us, like the tears in Magdalene's vial. It defines us and marks us and tells us what matters. And to let it go can feel like saying, "This doesn't matter to me anymore." But that's not what Jesus is asking. He is not asking us to let go of our identity or to deny what is precious to us or to say that our pain is unimportant. Letting go is a much more nuanced and liberating maneuver of heart than that. Instead, he is asking us to give him this most precious pain so he may put comfort in its place. He is asking us to anchor our identity in him, he who is able to redeem all pain, make it worthy, powerful, transformative, a force for good in the world and in us, to give it a proper and eternal horizon. He does this because he receives it perfectly, knows it completely, carries it entirely—easily—for us. He does this because he loves us so mightily.

I realize that to give him all my private agony—pain I bear, pain I've wrought, all my failings and my very broken heart—is to truly fall in love with him. It is to recognize him because he has called me by name so I might say, "Jesus, raise me from this sin-death. Rise in me." It is to accept his loving, clear command: "Don't cling to me; go and tell the others."

It was when he spoke her name that Mary Magdalene knew him, when he called her by her name, "Mary," that she fell at his feet and clung to him: "Rabboni!" When he came to her and met her in her mourning—one of the most intimate exchanges recorded in the Gospel. It was then that she got her assignment, to spread the extraordinary news of the Resurrection. It was then that she could say, "I have seen the Lord!" because he first saw her, knew her—in all sorrow and joy—and loved her completely.

When we fall in love with Jesus, this is exactly what it means: He meets us precisely where we are and calls us by name, and from there he draws us into the fullness of our true identity as redeemed by the resurrected one. And he sends us forth to tell the others, "We have seen the Lord."

At the anointing stone, I poured out blessed myrrh and nard, but I left some in the bottles to bring home. I have been divvying it up among friends and family, all the holier for having been present in so many sacred places in the Holy Land. I kept a small vial of myrrh for myself. Every morning, I bless my heart with it. Throughout the day, if my head tips down to read or write or pray, I can smell it—that fragrance that reminds me of death, and stillness, and searching for that one I love who loves me. The fragrance also reminds me of resurrection.

And I know with absolute certainty that I have been called by name too. I know with perfect clarity that I am known and loved and cherished, and all that is most precious to me is honored in heaven. And that I am to tell the others, "I have seen the Lord, and he is risen." I know as well and as deeply and sincerely as I have known anything in my life that it is my hour too, my Magdalene hour, when Jesus is raised and is raising my own heart.

Yes, Jesus, come. And rise.

Christ Encounter

Pray: As you settle into prayer, ask the Holy Spirit to guide your prayer and meditation.

Through the intercession of St. Mary Magdalene, pray with Luke 7:36–50.

Suggestions for meditation:

- What is Jesus doing in this passage?
- Where are you in the scene?
- Are there any sins that you withhold from Christ's forgiveness?
- Is there a payoff for hanging on to them?
- How might you give them to Jesus?
- Converse with him about this.

Write: What movements of heart took place in your prayer? What did Jesus do? How did you feel at the start and then at the end of your prayer?

Doxology: Give thanks for the prayer you have just experienced.

Questions for Small-Group Discussion

- Kelly makes reference to a vial of tears. What was the significance of this in New Testament times, and how does she apply it to us now?
- The theme of resurrection and new life is the great hope running through every Christian life. In what ways do you want to experience new life?

2

SHEPHERD GIRL

"'Talitha cum . . . little girl, get up!'"
—Mark 5:41

Like every other major lake in Minnesota, the one a few blocks from my front door has a "Lake Avenue." Along Lake Avenue, I ride my bike or walk the dogs and study the beautiful houses that line the shore. Mine is a former resort town for wealthy city dwellers, and many of the cottages here still reflect the Victorian era, when they were erected on large, wooded, breezy lots along the shore, perfect respite from city heat in the summer.

My Lake Avenue is somewhat elderly, a lush canopy of mature oaks and cottonwoods, their limbs sprawling overhead. The lake has receded in recent years, and this has created a fresh marsh area where a menagerie of birds congregates to sing—the more you listen, the better you can identify the call of each. Each song is unique, magnificent, tossed out over the cattails and pussy willows with a sweet, unselfconscious joy. Painters sometimes come and sit here with their easels. And nearby there's a small dog park where loping and happy hounds retrieve tennis balls thrown into the water. On the lake, sailboats tack to and fro; an occasional motorboat strikes out to find a favorite fishing hole. On a breezy day, parasails dot the sky.

Here, I can stretch my eyes to the horizon. Here, I can breathe.

Sometimes, I come to the water's edge to say my prayers. I sit on a bench and read and write and pray. I take a deep breath and listen to the waves and think, *Lord, I would give you this moment of rest, right here, right now, if I could.* I invite Jesus to come and sit with me, and in my imagination—he in a white robe and sandals and me in my sneakers and sun hat—we close our eyes and sit in silence together and listen to the birds and waves. I thank God for the horizon and wind, water, and sky, and for someone to sit with.

Lake Avenue slices a small, one-lane road between the beach houses and their beachfront yards. For one particular stretch, there's a bit of lush lawn. Here folks have situated their lounge chairs and grills and built charming gazebos and the occasional bunkhouse. Pontoons are anchored off their docks. In one beachfront yard, there is a play set for children, complete with slide and swing set. I am fond of this particular spot for the little girl who plays there. Maybe three or four, she plays with the kind of abandon that only a child well loved and secure could muster.

As I pass by on a particularly warm day, I notice that she has decided to play on the swing, but rather than sit on it, she has thrown her belly over the seat and drapes over it, dangling legs on one side and arms on the other. She sways and dangles, sways and dangles, the scene made more priceless by the fact that she is buck naked, her little brown bum—evidence that this is not the first time her rump has met the full sun—casually and without a care flashing the world that walks by on Lake Avenue.

I chuckle and think, *Unless you change and become like children, you will never enter the kingdom of heaven* (Matthew 18:3). Of course, the kingdom of heaven is not some sunny nudist colony (at least not to this aging body). But I do wonder about a kind of childlike, spiritual nakedness before the Lord—the kind that allows a child to assume safety and know that her caretaker is always nearby. The kind of childlike trust that is completely unselfconscious because this child has not yet been taught to condemn all the wrong things or get distracted by the superficial—it is the kind of presence that assumes love and total acceptance, the kind that rejoices at the sight of a present, that delights to be given every kind of gift and that trusts in goodness. The kind that, even though corrected or chastised by authority, immediately raises her arms in her distress and cries, "Daddy, hold me!"

Let me always be a child before you, Lord—your daughter.

Madeleine L'Engle once commented that if you cannot be fully three, you cannot be fully thirty-three or fifty-three or eighty-three. She said, "If we lose any part of ourselves, we are thereby diminished. If I cannot be thirteen and sixty-one simultaneously, part of me has been taken away."[1] Much has been written in recent years about reclaiming our "inner child" and the like. I don't know about reclaiming that child as much as integrating her. I can put away childish things without putting away the child and the important gifts she brings to me, the song she sings to me when my soul is most at rest, most abandoned to love. L'Engle said it this way:

> I need not belabor the point that to retain our childlike openness does not mean to be childish. Only the most mature of us are able to be childlike. And to be able **to be childlike involves memory; we must never forget any part of ourselves**. As of this writing I am sixty-one years old in chronology. But I am not an isolated, chronological numerical statistic. I am sixty-one, and I am also four, and twelve, and fifteen, and twenty-three, and thirty-one, and forty-five and . . . and . . .[2]

This is a matter neither of rejecting the child as having outgrown her nor of casting her off as though she were optional but rather of owning and integrating her, of reclaiming her innocence and preserving her childlike faith always before the Lord.

No child is a skeptic (no saint is a cynic!), and our culture doesn't appreciate that very much. It has become intellectually chic to be a naysayer. Our world has a tendency to crush childlike wonder and innocence. We learn not to trust the world, and often, as women, at a very early age, not to trust ourselves and the hopes we carry. But I am convinced that some big part of heaven, no matter our age or accomplishments, will always see us as daughters and relish our wonder and childlike trust.

Keeping Watch by Night

Some of my strongest childhood memories are of Christmastime. Saying the rosary as a family around our Christmas tree, attending midnight Mass, the countless Nativity plays and pageants that a family of seven children attending Catholic school would encounter. Our Nativity set was especially elaborate. My father built it from old barn wood, and, budding artist that I was, I was given the task of painting the figures: the wise men a mix of green and purple robes, Mary in blue, a shepherd in white.

Maybe because Christmas is about angels and babies and is the greatest "once upon a time" of all, it is easy for children to see themselves in the events of Jesus' birth. It touches something pure and unaffected in us, something forever youthful. To visit Bethlehem and Shepherds' Field in Israel was a kind of return for me, a time to revisit this radical innocent wonder. Walking the grounds, I sensed a healing restoration for every sin that I had committed against the delight of others or that had been committed against my childlike faith and delight in the Lord. I felt lighter and deeper, all at once.

Shepherds' Field is much like you might imagine it: quiet, peaceful, unassuming, a small, forgotten bit of remarkable history hovering over a very unremarkable bit of sloping, spotty pasture. Pine trees and caves clutter the hillside. There is visible evidence of the ongoing archaeological work, the great unearthing of a world long past. It's almost as if something very old and sleepy has been awoken. I have a picture in my head of one of the archaeologists gently waking a Rip Van Winkle shepherd to say, "Excuse me, sir, but I wonder if you might tell me the history of this place," and the shepherd rubs his eyes and sits up and begins the story, moving slowly through little details that most of us would miss, but the archaeologist, whose life is ordered by such ancient minutiae, catalogs every word.

The digs are subtle, slow procedures. I sense the enormous patience of those who work on them and the sincere respect that these scientists have for all that has come before them. And the wonder and delight they carry in their search. The delight in the looking, the searching and finding, the retrieving something that has long been lost. The delight in the reading of human history and the longings of man in the earth, the rocks and ruins.

We are told that shepherds would bring their flocks into caves like these for the night as protection against predators. One cave in particular, decorated with a fourth-century mosaic floor, has been reserved as a small chapel. Altar and pews have been formed out of the rock, and this is where we celebrate a quiet Mass, hidden and protected under the earth. It is fitting and humble.

But when the sound of our singing echoes against the hewn-rock walls, our voices are amplified, as though there were many more of us than there are. If you listen, if you're paying attention, you can feel it: that somewhere very near here, something sacred and dazzling and formidable and overwhelming hovered over these very hills. And there was music and light and a terrible glory that shook the earth and the hearts of men.

And you cannot help but wonder, *Lord Incarnate, why? Why did you come to us? As a man, as a child?*

In that region there were shepherds living in the fields, keeping watch over their flock by night (Luke 2:8).

I try to imagine night in an ancient land and myself in it, millennia before the mechanical hum of machines and motors entered the world. I try to think of the most natural quiet I have ever known, maybe after a fresh nighttime snow. Maybe the expectant hush that falls over the crowd as the houselights go down and the conductor raises his baton. Maybe a holy hour in the dead of night when it's just me and Jesus—that still quiet that is filled with presence, the holy, mystical touch of God.

When I close my eyes, I imagine I am one of the shepherds, the youngest of them, very little, nothing but a child, and the whole world exists for me, just as it does for all children.

The air is clear and chilly, and there is dew on the grass. I hear the faint movement of the herds, the soft night sounds of a world at rest. Herd animals have an aroma of their own at night; they take on the warm and reassuring smell of sleeping beasts—it is as though their very slumber has a fragrance. I am quiet and calm and at peace in all of this, even in my own nothingness. As it often does, my gaze turns toward the heavens, the glory of the stars, the vast, hovering universe stretching out over the fields, over me, and my mind is filled with a child's wonder.

Suddenly the sky erupts with light and singing. It is frightening, confusing, and I shield myself. *What could this be?* There are voices and beings, brightness beyond imagining, sounds I've never heard, and after some moments the sky goes dark again, the stars reappear, but nothing will ever be the same. A startled silence falls over the other shepherds and then I hear the word—though I barely know what it means: "angel."

Everyone starts running, and I cannot understand what is going on nor do I know where they are going, but I follow along with the others. What else would a child do?

It is dark but our feet fly. We are light and quick. We do not miss a step. Until in the distance I see we are approaching a cave—only it is illuminated, not cold, dark, damp but a warm, living, glowing sort of place. As we draw nearer, the other shepherds slow down, and when we are quite close, they stop and kneel. I kneel too. I think I should keep my head down but I want to sneak a glance. There is something—someone—ahead in that cave. Dare I look? A woman, a baby. *Didn't the angel say something of this, something of infants and that other word so inviting and mysterious, "savior"?*

We are captivated, speechless. Then one, the oldest and wisest of us, thinks to approach this woman, and the woman says, "Wait a moment," and then she turns to look directly at me. She gestures for me to come forward. And I can see the head shepherd is taken aback, confused by this, as if to say, "What could you possibly want with her?" He is a humble, good man, hardworking and honest; it's disorienting to see him confounded.

But I go. Though I have no sense of what is taking place or who she is, it seems I cannot resist her invitation to approach, and when I get closer, I see she's so beautiful and lovely and superb in every way. She smiles at me, and I draw nearer. We look down on the baby in her arms together.

I say, "He's so small."

And she says, "Yes, babies are very little."

"He's so soft," I say, and she smiles and nods. "He smells good," I say, and she laughs a little.

"Yes, so sweet," she says. Then somehow I am in her lap and so is the baby. She is holding me and I am holding him. And then he takes my finger—curls his little fist around my own child's finger—and squeezes. And I look at this beautiful woman and say, "Look! He's touching me."

Her whole expression changes, deepens, and she says, "Yes, he is."

He *is* touching me, touching my heart, in this prayer, in this meditation, and in that slightest connection, sending a world of healing, oceans of grace, a universe of glory pulsing through an infant's grip. *Child, how I love you!*

Then I remember the question I had been asking: "Why did you come? Why pour all your glory and power into one little baby?"

And he says to me, not in words, but through that little innocent fist, this helpless little creature, "So I could touch you, flesh of my flesh."

I believe him down to my bones.

Talitha cum

Anna, a wife and a mother to seven, a wise and prayerful woman, would like to be a writer. I suspect she already is. She feels called to this service and has for a long while. Writing has been with her since she was a child. She has been affirmed in this talent as a real charism on numerous occasions, and it is clear she desires to serve in this way, to find herself, to find her relationship with Jesus through pen and paper, and to bring others into deeper relationship with him through her writing. Her hunger for this has grown dramatically and unmistakably in recent years.

Slowly, circumstances align such that she can spend more time in prayer, more time in writing, more time in silence waiting on the voice of the Lord. Her children are all in school now, which leaves some writing room in her day. There's just one catch. She must give up a stressful, part-time accounting job—one she performs without pay, as a volunteer, for a worthy national ministry—to create more time and space for developing this much-needed charism of writing.

She's worried she will be letting people down if she gives up this work. She doesn't want to inconvenience or disappoint anyone. Like so many of us, she is somehow tempted by the lie that a blessing for her means a curse for someone else. She knows this is not how God works, but the persistence of this pernicious lie at the heart level takes some undoing.

We speak of this for more than a year in spiritual direction. Accounting is not one of her charisms, certainly not something she enjoys. Still there is resistance to be shed, self-doubt and insecurity to be redeemed and realigned in the light of Christ, concrete affirmation upon which to wait. This takes time and prayer. But then, like a sweet and gentle rain, things fall into place, washing away the doubt and fear and resistance. Her husband supports her decision. Out of the blue, another volunteer steps forward to help take over her volunteer duties. We make a plan for her resignation and the transition to a new accounting-support person. She schedules a three-day silent retreat to kick off this new phase of her life. The relief in her is palpable. Just thinking about giving up this work fills her with such relief, you can see it; her entire comportment changes. She sits up a bit and beams.

I look at her and think, *This is the work of the child. This is the touch of the infant.* Anna has given herself permission to be who she is, in Christ, and what a delight! We all win.

It can be done. You can become exactly the person you were meant to be in the Lord—ongoingly. The dream of the woman is often the dream of the child. And it is often the dream given you by the child Jesus.

Why do we so often resist it—the very thing Jesus wishes to give us, that deepest thing we desire?

I have no doubt that Jesus was an excellent carpenter. I'm certain some of his clientele were flummoxed by his decision to quit the workshop and travel and teach and preach. But the Father was calling the Child to something more. When the Father calls, we, as his children, long to answer, and we need a certain freedom to do so. L'Engle says that we must "let go our adult intellectual control and become as open as little children. This does not mean to set aside or discard the intellect, but to understand that it is not to become a dictator, for when it does we are closed off from revelation"[3]—that is, closed off from the very voice of the Father. Ultimately, I believe, we are closed off from love.

Rev. Gerald Vann, in his lovely book *The Divine Pity*, ties a childlike heart directly to holiness, calling it "the care-free spontaneity and uncalculating magnificence of gesture of the saints."[4] He continues: "It is that they are become, in truth, as little children, because they have learnt how the human reason may be perfected by the divine; they learnt how to judge instinctively with the eyes of God by living in the life of God; they have learnt that to be fully free you must become wholly obedient to the touch of the Spirit." Our adultness often works diligently against this docility.

But we know Jesus has an interest in resurrecting children and the docility in which they flourish. I think of the story of Jairus, who fell to his knees before Jesus. His only daughter was sick and near death. He begged Jesus to heal his precious daughter.

Jesus first attended to the crowds nearest him, and when the servants of Jairus reported that the child had died, Jesus told his disciples and the crowd, "Do not fear, only believe, and she will be saved," and later, "Do not weep; she is not dead, she is only sleeping." Their response was all too telling: they laughed at him. Note, it was the adults who were filled with doubt, the adults who said, "Nothing can be done now, the child is dead." Jesus ignored them. He knew what he was about. He took the little girl's hand and said, "Child, arise," *and her spirit returned.* The child was obedient to the touch of the Lord.

How often I long to take Jesus by the hand and go rescue the little child, to leave behind my doubts and cynicism and the adult dictator that wants to rule the child's heart. What will it take to give her permission to believe that she might rise and be restored in spirit?

As a Father Has Compassion for His Daughter

The Psalmist is clear:

> Bless the LORD, O my soul
> and all that is within me,
> Bless his holy name . . .
> and do not forget all his benefits—
> who forgives all your iniquity
> who heals all your diseases . . .
> who satisfies you with good as
> long as you live
> **so that your youth is renewed**
> like the eagle's . . .
> As a father has compassion for
> his children,
> so the LORD has compassion
> for those who fear him.

> —Psalm 103, emphasis added

In his compassion, the Lord loves to renew us, to bring about our delight and soul satisfaction.

Some years ago, I had the chance to live at the hobby farm my brother and parents keep. I was set to travel abroad for study and had about a month to spend before I left, so I was between housing situations. I was working on a book at the time, and in this delicious location, in this delicious month, I would spend the day praying and working on my book and then in the evening, I would take Shadow, my brother's black Arabian, out for a ride.

Riding, especially in the evening, has always been a prayerful experience for me—though as a child I would not have known to identify it that way. The sound and rhythm of hooves, the sun setting, some of the heat of the day subsiding, the crickets coming out, and the satisfaction of the day's work; I would think about what I'd written that day and pray and thank God for the incredible gift it was to live there for a while and to ride again. Those hours were filled with delight.

This time at the farm recalled the innocent delights of childhood: horses, sleigh and buggy, riding, cleaning tack, sweeping out the barn and the smell of oats and hay, mucking stalls, the little white half-moons that would fall on the barn floor when we trimmed hooves, grooming and combing out cockleburs, learning how to pick hooves, and training one of my horses from the day he was born. All of it—it was such an important gift and formed in me a deep love for the natural world. As I enter the last portion of my life, I realize more and more the great grace that was poured into me in those early days. My love for horses and farm life was a gift I shared in a heightened way with my dad.

One of the best parts of riding is coming home. The driveway at the farm is long and somewhat winding and runs parallel to a meadow. Just before you reach the barn, there is a last little rise before it breaks out into the yard. My habit was to canter up the last little hill and break over the crest of it. To feel the strength of the horse and hear his hooves on the soft earth, to feel the wind on my face and watch it blow through his mane—these were enchanted moments.

And to my delight, how often my father would be sitting there, waiting up on the porch, looking for me to break the crest of the hill, smiling, watching me come home. He loved to see me ride. It was a chance to delight in my delight. My delight and my father's delight were one. And our joy was magnified.

To use our gifts well, to delight in them as we do so, is precisely to ride up the crest of the hill and break through to find our way home. It is to make my will one with the Father's. As Rev. Vann writes:

> There is no excuse for a deliberate stunting of gifts of mind and character which God has given. You have to become a personality, to have a mind and will of your own; you have to learn to see and then to judge, you have to acquire the wisdom of the serpent as well as the simplicity of the dove. But then, in the second place, you have to preserve precisely that simplicity; you have to avoid the self-willed piety, the determination to decide at all costs for yourself what is right and wrong, the idea of the virtuous man as the self-made man, which turns virtue from worship of God into something very like worship of the self. **You must be able to listen with childlike simplicity to the voice of God and identify your own will with His**; then you need the strength and maturity of the grown [woman] in order to make your obedience to the voice not the obedience of a slave or an automaton but the creative gift of a lover.[5]

And the innocent gift of a child.

The little child believes in delight. The little girl knows that her delight brings delight to her Father. And when we listen for that delight, when we lose ourselves in our gifts, something of heaven spills into this earthly life.

Passion Child

Some years ago, my parents and I decided to spend Easter Mass at my brother's weekend parish, St. Vincent de Paul, which serves the Hmong of our community. Some of the Mass was conducted in Hmong, a tonal language—that is, the tone, like a musical pitch, is used to determine the meaning of words. I was impressed by this feature of the language and the intricacy involved, especially when my brother said some parts of the Mass in Hmong.

I was also struck by the lack of pretention in this strongly familial culture. The congregation was extraordinarily hospitable and inviting, warm, and real. There was a respect for their elders that was beautifully apparent and, bubbling just under the surface of it all, a deep delight in the children.

After Easter Mass, they hosted a large banquet and offered several celebratory presentations, including a Passion play put on by the preschoolers. The children marched out in front of the audience with handwritten name tags pinned to their shirts to indicate their roles: "Jesus," "Bad guy," "Good thief," and so on. The teacher stood behind them with a microphone, narrating and directing the little troupe.

When she got to the line "Then Jesus was arrested by a bad guy," "Jesus," a gorgeous little boy in a bright blue shirt and black vest, popped to his feet, his face beaming, and he placed his hands behind his back in anticipation of his arrest. When the "bad guy" had placed him in make-believe handcuffs, Jesus was marched off to Pilate, and then to the Cross, stretching out his tiny, perfect little child's arms—all the while his face beaming.

To live in heaven's delight, to do the will of the Father, to discover, develop, and then offer our charisms in service, does not mean that we get to skip the work of the Cross. Far from it. Every charism, every vocation, bears the imprint of the Cross; every path to holy delight has buried deep within it the terrible joy of the Via Dolorosa and three hours' brutal crucifixion on a Friday afternoon. We might like to imagine that Jesus on the Cross was somehow tough, rugged, "taking it like a man," when in fact he was taking it like an innocent. That same child-Jesus who would squeeze my little finger and trust in me, depend on me to hold him safely in my arms, would also die for me. All of Jesus went to the Cross. There was something of that holy child at play that was crushed for our iniquities. This truth must blaze through every vocation, every charism, every gift we make to the Lord and to one another.

But another truth burns along with it: When three days had passed, his Father reached down and took his hand, and said, "Child, arise!" And the spirit of the Lord returned.

This is precisely the same hand extended to you. When the world and sin ask you to forget the little girl, tell you she is dead and there is nothing to be done, let the child Jesus take your hand, wrap his little infant arms around you, and bring you into heaven's delight.

For my father, Richard, on Father's Day, 2016

Christ Encounter

Pray: As you settle into prayer, ask the Holy Spirit to guide your prayer and meditation.

Through the intercession of the Holy Innocents, pray with Mark 5:35–42.

Suggestions for meditation:

- What is Jesus doing in this passage?
- Where are you in the scene?
- Is there resistance to "rising"?
- Is there a moment when you remember your dreams were crushed?
- Can you invite Jesus into this moment?
- Converse with him about this.

Write: What movements of heart took place in your prayer? What did Jesus do? How did you feel at the start and then at the end of this prayer?

Doxology: Give thanks for the prayer you have just experienced.

Questions for Small-Group Discussion

- Do you remember a time when you were completely delighted, like a child, before the Lord? What was the occasion?
- Jesus encourages us to become like a child that we might enter his kingdom. In what ways do you struggle to become more childlike?

3

MOTHER

There are not only Fathers of the Church, but also Mothers of the Church.

—Hanna-Barbara Gerl-Falkovitz

My mom and I have come to the North Shore of Lake Superior to sit in a little cabin and look out across the water and pray with the waves and the wind. We will rest and take a stroll now and then, and I will write and ask my mom's advice and counsel—she has a remarkably fine editorial ear—and we will enjoy the peace of being together, just the four of us: Mom, me, the lake, and the Lord.

In her eighties now, though in fine health by all accounts, she slows more and more. It takes her longer to get up from a chair and get moving, her short-term memory has become a source of gentle humor, and she is very content to simply sit and pray her novenas or read *The Poem of the Man-God* by Maria Valtorta. And I take note of the quiet shift that has been taking place over the years—from the entrustment of my care to her to the entrustment of her care to me. And I am humbled at the graceful rhythm of this shift that has been ordained by the Maker of All.

I hope every woman is as lucky as I have been in this: there are more than a few times in my life when I knew my mother was an absolute genius, but one moment stands out.

When I was about twelve, my father was elected judge, a position that would require us to move. We would leave the country and my childhood home—the farm, the barn, my beloved horses—and live in a new city. I was heartbroken. I'll never forget the day a neighboring family came to pick up our horses.

It was early spring in Minnesota. Spring in the country is a magnificent thing, tantalizing every sense. Most of the snow has melted, and the sun slowly warms the fields as they emerge from so many buried months. Soil in the spring in Minnesota has its own distinct scent, and the air was filled with the promise of growing things, a future warm with hope.

But my heart was like a stone. I helped assemble the tack, the buggy and sleigh—all of the things that were my childhood world—and prepared to give them to the family that was taking ownership. They were a good, solid family with good farm kids. I knew they would be kind to our horses, but the loss I felt was still immense. When you're a child, sometimes God's creatures help to make sense of the nonsensical; they help you to survive unimaginable pain. Like the day a classmate's mother, in a state of psychosis, murdered her baby girl and threw her out the window. Driving home from the funeral, my mom simply said, "Why don't you go for a ride when you get home." I'll never forget that ride. These days a mother might feel pressured to schedule therapy treatments or force a conversation about feelings. Instead, my grief and confusion were met with the sheer maternal genius in simply allowing a child space to grieve and seek solace in the barn.

It is important to talk sometimes, and naming feelings can be a tremendous help to us as we move through the especially difficult ones. But sometimes, motherhood isn't about the words coming out of your mouth but the love—and restraint—offered from your heart.

I watched as one of the young boys rode my horse—a horse I'd trained and known from its first breath—away across the fields, away from home. He was a gentle animal and would not make a fuss, but he looked back at me, clearly confused, as if to say, "Who is this guy, and why aren't you coming with us?" He was only green broke, and I was the only person who had ever ridden him. To my twelve-year-old heart, I might as well have been handing over my own child.

I held it together until they were maybe half a mile from the farm. Then I slumped down in the hallway and wept uncontrollably. It was one of the most painful moments of my childhood.

And my mother allowed me to experience it in full. She knew—more than anyone else—just exactly what I was losing that day, and she didn't fix it, didn't try to control it, did not try to make me feel better, didn't even say a word. She simply stood over me with her hand on my head and wept with me, and I think that there was something of the purest kind of mothering in her response. There are times when it simply cannot be made better, but it can be witnessed in such a way that growth is inevitable. The balm is in the witnessing without an agenda. Mothers are called upon to do a great deal of witnessing while setting aside their own hopes. And like Mary at the foot of the Cross, much of that is painful, even when it is good.

The Mysteries of Motherhood

On a day retreat I was leading for a group of women, one approached me during the break. I had noticed her slip in and sit in the front row. She was lovely, well put together, but her face held a certain strain.

"Father suggested I come talk to you," she said. I had just finished a talk on suffering as a mercy and gift from God, how "suffering unleashes love" in the world and in our families. We went in search of a quiet place, and the story unfolded.

Her young husband had been diagnosed with a terrible disease that required extreme treatments—and that might take his life. They had four young children.

"Everything you said," she said weakly, "I get that for myself. I'm on board with all of it for myself"—and she could barely finish the thought, "but for my kids . . ."

Becoming a mother changes every experience a woman will have. Every event will in some way be measured against how it may or may not affect her child. One friend described it this way: "When I had my first child, I suddenly realized that my heart would be marching around open and exposed and vulnerable in the world for the rest of my days." Motherhood, in all its colors and variety, invokes a kind of selflessness that little else does.

Before I even began this chapter, I realized my own limitation of never having had children myself. I've spent a great deal of time, though, with theology and philosophy on the subject of motherhood, both physical and spiritual. One of the courses I teach in Catholic studies is Woman and Man: Philosophical Issues. I can quote some of the great minds on the subject. And there are great minds to be quoted. I especially love what Romano Guardini has to say about motherhood and how he links it directly to the Eucharist:

> The gift of the Eucharist and our Lord's death are, in the deepest sense, one and the same mystery. The love that drove Him to die for us was the same love that made Him give us Himself as nourishment. It was not enough to give us gifts, works, and instructions; He gave us Himself as well.
>
> Perhaps we must seek out woman, the loving mother, to find someone who understands this kind of longing: to give not some *thing*, but rather oneself—to give oneself, with all one's being; not only the spirit, not only one's fidelity, but body and soul, flesh

and blood, everything. This is indeed the ultimate love: to want to feed others with the very substance of one's own self.[6]

The whole world cries out for this kind of mothering: that substantial self-giving—or at the very least, "remothering." It is not only important on the natural level; as John Paul II would point out, "Motherhood has been introduced into the order of the Covenant that God made with humanity in Jesus Christ. *Each and every time that motherhood is repeated in human history, it is always related to the Covenant* which God established with the human race through the motherhood of the Mother of God."[7] Far from being a limitation of a woman's flourishing, the church recognizes motherhood in every instance, in every pregnancy, as a harbinger of the greatest story ever told and as a sign that points to God's extraordinary and loving intervention: the Incarnation. And it is precisely from this event that every mother may draw new strength.

The joy of this cannot be lost on any mother. The Incarnation was the coming of the Messiah, but it was also the birth of a baby. The answer to all the fears, hopes, and anxieties in the heart of a people rested on a baby—and therefore on his mother. John Paul says, "Do we not find in the Annunciation at Nazareth the beginning of that definitive answer by which God himself 'attempts to calm people's hearts,'" in the anticipation of the birth of a child?

Motherhood is not an uncomplicated affair; it certainly wasn't for the Blessed Mother or for the countless barren women of the Bible God decided to make fertile, even in old age. Motherhood has always been more mystery and less mysticism. It is constituted more of hard work, self-sacrifice, and patience, and less of basking in the love of grateful, well-formed, adoring, perfectly healthy and accomplished children who make perfect decisions that are deeply pleasing to a mother's heart and exactly what she hoped for them. To mother well, unique skills might be needed for each child. From where I stand, mothering seems to have grown even more complex in recent years. There are the challenges of being a single mother, a working mother, a mother who is ill; the problem of infertility or having sick children; and the difficulties of navigating everything from breast-feeding to learning disabilities, peer pressure, and college applications. Our children are assaulted by drugs, pornography, and wild immorality flaunted as the norm—and moms are held accountable at every turn.

And there are different kinds of motherhood; every woman places her own unrepeatable, unique stamp upon it. Every woman feels her own wound from it. In the following pages, you will meet just a few of the souls who help make up the motherhood of the church. I could have filled volumes. It was genuinely painful to pick and choose which interviews to include. I am deeply grateful to these generous women for their candor and courage, their thoughtfulness, and their willingness to plumb the depths of the mysteries of motherhood.

Angela: The Little Inn

Angela, an intelligent, thoughtful, prayerful young person, had always dreamed of being a wife and mother. She grew up with a passion for making a home.

"The duties of homemaking were something I just naturally loved," she said. "I loved to clean, I loved to cook, I loved creating a home."

Married now going on three years, she got pregnant essentially on her honeymoon and gave birth to baby John ten months after her wedding. She characterizes her experience of marriage and motherhood thus far in one striking theme: "I've been trying to find Christ in the desert."

It was in the year or two prior to marriage—a period she intentionally dedicated to prayer and no dating—that she began to sense a very particular call, even within the vocation of marriage: "to restore the church by restoring the family," she said. "It's a very hidden call, not something that anyone else would necessarily see, but in my own hidden life, I felt called to sanctifying the home and the family."

But it seemed that, almost the moment she got married, the passion for homemaking and homelife disappeared.

"All of a sudden, my love for cooking was just gone," she said. "My love for cleaning, all of these things that even in a natural way I loved to do, they just were gone. And they've never really come back . . . even into motherhood. . . . Spiritually speaking, it has been a lot of dryness and very desertlike."

Needless to say, this came as an entirely unexpected disappointment to Angela. And it did not relent.

"We all have normal times of dryness," Angela reasoned, "but this has been lasting so long that I started to question myself. Maybe I'm doing something wrong, maybe I offended the Lord, and I got worried that he was displeased with me because I also tend toward perfectionism. 'You have to be perfect to be loved.'"

She found solace and clarity in reading about the dark night of the senses as described by St. John of the Cross: how the soul suddenly struggles to want to pray or frequent the sacraments, how the person might wonder if he or she has done something wrong or offended the Lord. A first response might be to try harder, but John recommends trying to rest in the Lord's love.

"Whether I have experienced [the dark night of the senses] at all, I have taken on the principle of just trying to rest in the Lord's love. Even in the dryness."

Her Lenten prayer provided a particularly powerful way to manifest this rest. Instead of focusing on giving up something she liked—though she did that, too—she focused on giving up her perfectionism. Where she might have been tempted to berate herself for forgetting to plan dinner, for example, she would intentionally remind herself, "It is not what I do that makes the Lord love me; it's simply that he loved me into being and that his love is what sustains me."

"It was like a single prayer throughout Lent, a single thought that I would try to return to frequently to find a way to rest in him. It was easy to compare myself to other mothers who have their house all put together and seem to have this rich spiritual life and seem able to do it all, and here I am struggling to clean my house once a week. . . . I was trying to . . . concretely let go of those comparisons and those judgments of myself. Just come back to the fact that the Lord loves me simply because of who I am."

This simple approach paid off.

"It was very freeing," she said. "I think it was the best Lent I've ever had. It was so simple and in some ways so ordinary. There was nothing austere about my particular fast, but it was exactly what I needed."

Like many young mothers, and especially young Catholic mothers who struggle in a culture that sometimes openly mocks them for staying home to raise their children or for having a large family, she struggled with a romanticized view of motherhood.

"I used to get filled with jealousy when I saw young women with babies," she said. "I was sensitive to the 'I want a baby crave'. . . . It's such a romanticized view of what it's like to care for a baby, because you only see the baby when it's cute and not fussing and you've had a great night's sleep. I just always thought that I would love caring for children and find it so fulfilling."

It was disheartening to Angela to feel otherwise.

"Looking back on the struggles I've faced in motherhood," Angela said, "I really thought it would just be very natural, raising a child. . . . Finding that it is not has contributed to the desert and darkness of it."

"I think I romanticized stay-at-home motherhood, too," she said. "I miss going to work. I miss seeing other people and exercising my intellect in that way . . . so it can be kind of lonely when you're spending sunup to sundown with a baby and the baby is adorable for two hours but the rest of the day you're changing diapers and cleaning spit up. . . . There's almost like this consolation painted over motherhood."

Blooming in the Desert

The desert, of course, is filled with many quiet splendors, and Angela has been discovering new joys in being a mother, even in dryness. Letting go of perfectionism and an unrealistic idealism, letting go of judging others, especially other struggling mothers, becoming more realistic about what's truly important. And more than anything, her child, baby John, has been opening her eyes to beauties all around her.

"One of the greatest gifts that John has given me is the gift of wonder at the world and the created order," she said.

She recalls her fondness for a class she took in graduate school about stewardship and sustainability. That course emphasized the need to "behold" and all that such a notion implies.

"Before we can talk about how to use the natural order and how to live as good stewards of the earth," she said, "we have to imitate the Lord in beholding the world as very good. How do you do that?" It turns out the real professor in this course of learning was baby John.

"We've become big birders," she recalled laughing. "Right out in our backyard is a wetlands restoration project. Standing at the window and beholding these birds is incredible. I was here a year and a half before I noticed my first bird, and it was because of John. He would look outside and *ooh* and *ahh* over the birds. John has actually made me 'stop and smell the roses' and helped me to learn the names of things. In order to love something, you have to know what it is, and so we name things."

Angela is now expecting fraternal twins, a girl and a boy. And just as parenting different children is different, her pregnancies have been very different.

"With John it was just joy and elation, even in the dryness, it was so wondrous to have a child grow in my womb. This pregnancy I have much more experienced the sacrifice of giving my body to these two children. I'm much bigger, and it's much more uncomfortable. There is the added anxiety that twin births are always considered higher risk." That has added to some of the desert experience, but it has also deepened her understanding of motherhood, prayer, and the mysterious ways in which the Lord chooses to love us.

"Christ gave us himself in his body and blood because he loves us," she said, "and I'm sure there's joy in that, but it's not as though it is *just* joyful. There is sacrifice, legitimate pain. We tend to forget that part."

Even in this dark night of the senses, she does have a hidden sense of growing closer to the Lord and to the Blessed Mother. She recalled a sermon in which the priest suggested that Advent was the time to form our hearts into little homes for the infant Jesus to dwell in, an image that struck a deep chord.

"Forming a little inn in our hearts has always resonated with me," Angela said. "With ultrasound, you can see so much more of what is going on [in pregnancy], but the whole process is still very hidden from us. You are creating this space inside you for a child to grow, but you don't actually meet the child until he is born. It requires real faith—that this child is growing and developing and you continue to nourish your body as best you can, so that it remains a hospitable place for the child."

She continued: "Similarly, you can ask yourself, 'Are you there, Jesus? Do you like it in there [in my heart]?' Just like the child in the womb, you can't really ask, 'How are you guys doing in there? Will you just kick me so I know you're in there?' You don't have a constant window there, so you seek to nourish them and trust that they are growing well. In a similar way, you are doing that with your faith and with prayer. We aren't always going to know, or be given the feedback that everything is well. Giving Christ the room to grow in us is actually quiet and hidden, but it doesn't mean that nothing is happening. Even when it's quiet and seemingly empty, it is often in those times that the Lord is working and growing in you the most."

Ruth: A Feast of Conception

Pretty, independent, and highly intelligent, Ruth was a serious Catholic with a promising future when she discovered that she was pregnant. It was her last semester of undergraduate studies. Her first reaction was utter disbelief and denial: she had been sexually assaulted by a man she was dating.

"I was trying to live what I would call a double life," she remembered. "I had been in denial about the whole relationship for several weeks and was telling myself that I loved this man and that we were going to get married. When he assaulted me, it just kind of sealed the deal of me trying to normalize the whole relationship, which was dysfunctional from the start."

Looking back nearly a decade, she readily recognizes the relationship as abusive, but at the time, as it often is in the middle of a struggle, things were much murkier. When reality about the pregnancy began to sink in, she decided to inform the biological father.

"He immediately pressured me very heavily to have an abortion," Ruth said. "And out of that, thankfully, in two or three days, as I started to actually be more honest with myself, I started reaching out to people I knew would hold me accountable."

Describing herself as "the most pro-life person in the world," she was still frightened that if she didn't let her close friends and family know what was happening, she might be manipulated.

"I was very scared," she said, "and even though I would never contemplate an abortion, to be honest, I was afraid that somehow the baby's father would wear me down if I didn't reach out to others."

So that's what she did. Ruth had been part of a strong Catholic community at her university. While the fear of judgment was very much on her mind, she was more determined to protect the life growing inside her. So, one by one, she let people in. To her relief, instead of being met with shame and recriminations, she was met with sincere support and genuine concern.

"Everyone around me was so generous and loving and not judgmental." It was also by being honest with her close friends and family that she could confront the abuse and end the relationship.

"They started to say, 'Ruth, you are trying to normalize the situation, but you have to look at the fact that you were assaulted and that was not healthy.'" She filed a police report, and, after a university investigation, her former boyfriend was kicked out of school.

A step in the right direction, certainly, but there was much more healing ahead.

"I had always wanted to be a mother," Ruth said. "I always thought I would get married and have children. So figuring out how to accept being pregnant and a mother—this was something I really wanted—but not in the way or at the time that I wanted it. That was really difficult."

The man she had been dating had been emotionally abusive, filling her with self-doubt and deep insecurity. To her surprise, the pregnancy began to unravel those lies and assuage her fears.

"Being pregnant, I grew in confidence," she recalled. "[I realized] I can do something really beautiful; my body is designed to do this amazing thing."

Now she can say with conviction, "I firmly believe I would not be where I am now in terms of how I have healed and grown if I hadn't gotten pregnant. My daughter is the greatest, best gift God has ever given me. It took being pregnant and experiencing that gift of life to be able to heal."

Her pregnancy and motherhood also strengthened her relationship with the Virgin Mary.

"I turned to the Blessed Mother immediately, especially when I was trying to decide whether I should parent or not." Her answer came on an especially meaningful Marian feast day.

"The day I finally felt confident in deciding to keep my baby was December 8, the Feast of the Immaculate Conception, and that was really significant to me because I thought, 'Mary is guiding me through this.' I had a strong sense that, because of her intercession, I could be confident about making a choice that was extremely hard for me to make."

She also credits her motherhood with reestablishing her relationship with Christ and her complete dependence on him. "Before I got pregnant, I was used to being able to do things really well on my own. Being pregnant and being a single mom, I had to give up [a sense of control]; I could not do it on my own. I had to rely, not only on other people, but also on God to sustain me in a way that I had never encountered before."

Being a single mother was one challenge. Other fears crept through her mind too. "I was afraid of the possibility that I would look at my daughter and see the face of someone I didn't want to see," she said. "But from the moment I had her, I have only seen Sophia for who she is, and she actually looks a lot like me, so that's really cool."

"There was the overwhelming sense that this is what I was made for, holding my child in my arms and feeling that God has given me this gift to be a mother and has given me this beautiful child, who has perfection written all over her."

Ruth lived with her mother and strung together a series of jobs that would allow her to stay home most of the time to be with her daughter. The church became a source of unfailing spiritual support. "I had a great deal of consolation in the sacraments and in the community of the faithful. The church is the vehicle of the sacraments, and when things have been hardest, going to the adoration chapel and receiving the Eucharist at Mass have been the most life-giving things for me."

And in time, she would open herself to the possibility of a relationship. "It took me a long time to feel confident in myself again, at least several years. I needed to grow into myself, and by the time I met [my husband, Matthew], I was really comfortable with myself."

Marriage has of course changed things. There is new delight in seeing her daughter flourish in the fullness of parenthood. "The day we got married, Matthew became Sophia's dad, and they love each other so much. It's beautiful to see how she is different with a father. He does so many things that I can't. Motherhood is wonderful, but I can't be a father. That has helped me tone down. As a single mom, I was able to make all the decisions and do things my way. Getting married and having another parent in the picture has forced me to hold back a little bit. Sometimes he parents differently. I need to respect his autonomy."

Not long after their marriage, Ruth became pregnant and miscarried just eleven and a half weeks later, revealing some health issues that may make it difficult to have more children. The contrast of how Sophia's biological father responded to Sophia's conception and how Matthew responded to the miscarriage is far from lost on Ruth.

"Miscarrying was one of the things that brought Matthew and me together the most," she said. "We went through this grief together, and he cared for me so well through the miscarriage. It was good to know that something so difficult brought us together in such a significant way."

The arc of her experience in pregnancy, motherhood, healing, and marriage has been compelling evidence to her of just how much God loves her. "It is precisely in my weakness, my humanity, and my failures that Christ comes and works in my life. Even now, dealing with infertility, it's just another reminder that I do not have control. Even when my desires are for good things. There's just so much out of my control, and God works in all of that—the messiness, the sins, the mistakes that we make."

"Having Sophia and marrying Matthew, I see both of those as very specific places where God has worked in those precise difficulties to bring about great good."

And to a woman who might find herself in similar circumstances, pregnant when she may not want to be for whatever reason, Ruth encourages taking time and thought in mapping a way forward.

"You are a mother," she said. "That's a beautiful gift, even when it's difficult or unwanted or unplanned. I'd encourage her to recognize that she has some choice in how to live with that gift now . . . and to consider adoption. It's one of the most loving, generous things any person can do. To give life to a child and then place that child in the arms of some other couple. . . . Any woman who is pregnant is a mother, no matter what happens in the future; even if she miscarries, she is still a mother to that child for all eternity. So even when it seems impossible or difficult or scary, to be able to give the gift of life to a child, it's a great privilege for a woman to be able to participate in that."

Only days after our interview, Ruth learned she was expecting her second child.

Grace: One Good Friday in Russia

Grace is an attractive, energetic woman with a great sense of style. She has a beautiful home, and when I'm walking through it, it is impossible to miss the most important person in Grace's life: pictures of her daughter, Margaret, are everywhere.

A successful businesswoman, Grace always wanted to be a mom, but life circumstances never quite presented marriage and family. It wasn't until two of her younger sisters were expecting at about the same time that she began to seriously consider adoption as a single woman. She was forty-three years old.

She recalls: "I projected forward and thought, what's it going to be like for you to see them with their children?" and she began to wonder whether it was too late for her to become a mother. After some rigorous investigation and thought, she decided to pursue adoption in Russia. The whole process took only fourteen months and was uncharacteristically smooth.

The first time Grace saw Margaret was on a Good Friday in a fairly remote Russian town. She had traveled two days to get there and had barely a moment's rest before the agency took her to the orphanage to meet the child they had selected for her on the basis of her profile.

Grace was escorted into what she described as a beautiful, very clean playroom filled with toys, books, colorful flowerpots, and lots of sunny windows. Then a nurse in a white lab coat came in carrying a little girl, just eleven months old.

"She was so small!" recalled Grace. "I knew she was eleven months old, but I just thought she'd be bigger. She was so tiny and delicate."

She sat down with the nurse, a translator, and a doctor. After a few minutes of introduction, the nurse asked Grace if she'd like to hold the child.

"She sat perfectly still in my lap," Grace remembers smiling, "and kind of looked over her shoulder at me, like, 'Who are you?' She was holding a toy giraffe." Then the others left the room, leaving Grace and Margaret alone for the first time.

"I picked up some blocks and started clapping them together, and I said to her, 'Look,' and she immediately looked over at me, and then she started to imitate me. I just started crying. I could tell that she was happy and that she was very resilient and had a strong spirit. She loved the attention and she responded to it. She was not a sorrowful child at all. I fell in love with her right away. Immediately."

Grace went home to wait for her court date in Russia and in the meantime added a room to her house. Then there was a longer return trip to Russia; she and a friend who accompanied her lived in a hotel for three weeks. After one week, Grace brought Margaret back with her to the hotel. She could sense that a bond had already been established.

"I think Margaret knew this was a permanent thing." Grace recalled that in her first night home in the United States, Margaret fell asleep in her crib as if she had done so a thousand times before.

"The next morning," Grace remembered, "I got up, I made her pancakes, we did laundry and played and played." Grace's family came to visit, and Margaret jumped right in and played with her two little cousins who were about her age.

"She knows who she is," Grace said, smiling. "Margaret has always known who she is."

"After we had been home for a few days, we would stand in front of the mirror and I would take my hand and point to her image in the mirror and say 'Margaret' and then I would tap my image and say 'Mama.' At fifteen months she was on the cusp of speaking a lot of Russian. After about three weeks, her first English word was 'hi' and then 'kitty' and then 'mama.' She called me 'Mama' after being home about one month."

Grace, who had been raised predominantly Episcopalian though had been baptized as a Catholic, was not particularly religious. But when Margaret came along, Grace's interest in religion slowly rekindled.

"I really believe that it was through my daughter that I was brought back into my Catholic faith. Absolutely. I absolutely believe that Margaret was part of the plan to get me back into the church and have a major conversion moment when I absolutely changed my life. She was a big part of that."

When Margaret was two years old, Grace had her baptized. When it came time for preschool, the local Catholic church had an elementary school and an opening. The fate of Grace and Margaret was sealed.

"Three months after she started preschool," Grace recalled, "we walked into church for Mass, and that was it. I had walked past that church and that campus hundreds, if not thousands, of times in the eighteen years I've lived here, and it had never once occurred to me—a baptized Catholic—to walk in. We went into Mass and there was benediction. It was opening day of the adoration chapel. The bishop was there, we processed around the school. . . . It was profound, beautiful, I loved it. And I thought, 'We're coming back next Sunday.' My reasoning was, it's beautiful, it's good for Margaret, I want her to be exposed to religion, she is in a Catholic school now. That was my starting point; it was about her and about my being a good role model."

As the weeks went by and as Easter came, Grace started to meet and talk with some of the other moms at the school. "Witnessing how other moms there were living and how Christ was the center of their lives, that was really compelling to me," said Grace.

She was invited to join their moms' group, and on her first visit, she was asked to tell her story and describe her faith. She explained that she had been confirmed in the Episcopal Church, but one of the other mothers recommended she go through the Rite of Christian

Initiation for Adults and get confirmed in the Catholic Church. About the same time, Grace picked up Matthew Kelly's *Rediscovering Catholicism*, which she notes was perfect for her at the time for its simplicity. Once Margaret reached kindergarten, Grace was in the habit of stopping into the church every day after dropping her off for school.

"I sat in the back of the church every day and thought how much I was changing: I was on my way to being confirmed, I was meeting all these Catholics, I was becoming very pro-life, whereas before I thought, 'It's a woman's choice.' Things were rapidly changing, and I knew there was no turning back. If this was going to be a genuinely deep conversion, I needed to be fully in."

Every day on her visits to the church she would simply ask, "Show me the way. What is your will for my life?'" One evening, as Grace was leaving her RCIA class, the instructor made a simple comment to her. "She told me 'Remember, Grace, as Jesus says, I am the way, the truth and the life,' and I thought to myself, there's my answer. I've been asking him to show me the way, and he's telling me, 'I am the way, follow me.' I've heard that verse my whole life and it never struck me before the way it did that night. Right then—that was a real breakthrough moment. I realized that not only was he speaking through this woman, but that now he must become front and center of my life."

It wasn't a perfectly seamless reordering. One hurdle was trying to reconcile loving Jesus before all others, even her daughter.

"I kept thinking, 'I can't love you more than I love Margaret. You're asking too much.' It wasn't until I really prayed about it that I realized that as with every Christian, it is by putting Christ first that you can love others more. Once that clicked, I said, okay, absolutely. And I realized too that he's initiating everything; it's right that he should come first."

Then came confirmation. "Easter Vigil was very powerful," Grace said. "When [the bishop] put his hands on my head, I thought it would be nice, but I didn't expect to feel the rush of the Holy Spirit on me. I didn't expect to feel something akin to hot warm honey pouring down my head. It was very sensory, very powerful."

Grace was home.

The Mary Effect

In the fervency of those early days reengaging her faith, Grace recalled that she was very involved and "it was all about Christ, Christ, Christ."

"I didn't really heed Mary," she said. "I didn't know how to incorporate her; I didn't know how she fit into it. What she did was wonderful, honorable, courageous, but she's not Christ; she's not divine." This was not an uncommon hesitation for many converts, but that wouldn't be the last word.

One spring, everything broke open for her with respect to the Blessed Mother.

"It came about through a deep flaw that I have: impatience. On this particular day, I had lost my patience with my beautiful, wonderful daughter in a really awful, saddening way for me. We went to Mass after the blowup and I sat there feeling dead inside. I felt myself caving in to despair. Margaret kept looking at me, saying, 'Mama, what's wrong?'"

Consumed with desolation, Grace did not go up to receive communion. After Mass, she went home, went to her room, and cried. She was aware that she was giving in to the temptation to despair.

"Yes, what I said to my daughter in the blowup was awful, but now I'm thinking my sin is bigger than God's forgiveness, [that] God will never forgive me."

As it happens, she was in charge of the altar linens that week and had forgotten them earlier. She went back to the church to get them. By that time, the church was empty and quiet. She looked down the aisle, and there at the end was a kneeler in front of a row of blue flickering candles situated at the feet of a statue of the Blessed Mother.

"I said, 'It can't hurt, I have to do something.'" So she knelt in front of Mary, and the moment she did, she noticed that all the candle flames had become stock-still. They burned brightly, but they did not move at all.

"I didn't know what to make of it, but it was very unusual," she recalled. "I just started praying to Mary, 'Lend me your heart. Please help me, I'm a mess. I'm so frightened.' I started sobbing, crying out for her help: 'I'm failing as a mother, I'm failing in my faith.' I went on and on and on. And then I had a sense of her presence coming over me and saying, 'It's okay, God loves you, Jesus loves you, you will be forgiven, your faith is your own, your daughter loves you, go back to her, go home, you are deeply loved.' It was Mary comforting me, telling me that her son loves me."

Filled with gratitude and relief, she returned home, ran to her daughter, begged her forgiveness, and asked if they could begin again.

"And we did," Grace said. "We went on a picnic that day. It was a new beginning."

That moment made a lasting impression, and Grace grew in her devotion to and dependence on the prayers of the Blessed Mother. And there were more gifts too.

"I've realized since then," she said, "that it's in your suffering that Jesus really does all the deep work, not in all your good works and how admired you are, but what you stumble upon that will bring you closer to Christ. So thank God for my impatience. It's right there, in that catch, in that thing that frustrates me so much, that thing that I can't seem to completely put to rest. That impatience . . . is bringing me closer to Christ."

Motherhood has been teaching her many things, stretching her in new ways in many virtues: patience, humility, selflessness. "To try to understand what being selfless is. Not losing myself but giving myself. Jesus did not lose himself [to us], he gave himself to us."

Grace has continued to throw herself into more study of her faith, completing a certificate in the study of the catechism and expanding her understanding through studies of the early church.

"My faith is a gift," she said, smiling, "and I believe it was all brought to me through this little girl."

Miriam: The Matter of Motherhood

Miriam is a tall, beautiful woman with a graceful stride. She holds herself with a certain elegance that's impossible to miss. Her voice is warm, and there is a depth to her that is apparent at once, the kind of depth that recalls being remade, and the kind of dazzling compassion that often accompanies such a journey.

A grandmother now, she currently works in a crisis pregnancy center, work she began not long after a routine visit to the grave of her fifth child, Joseph, who lived just one day and died in her arms nearly thirty years ago.

"I go to his grave at least once a year," she said. As it happens, very near his grave is a tombstone marker for thirteen unborn babies. It is etched with the words "Father, forgive them for they know not what they do." Those babies had been found in a dumpster near a place where abortions were performed.

"Here I am, grieving at the grave of my son," she remembered solemnly, "but also having had two abortions in 1972—it brought me back to that pain. And I just looked around and saw all the tombstones of the babies that were loved and then all those babies that were aborted and I just felt that I had to do something."

She weighed carefully her entrance into such work.

"I suffered a great deal because of the talk of Christians about women who'd had abortions," she said, "and I wasn't going to come close to that. But I told God I wanted to do something. I thought I could make a difference." Her work has taught her that the people who come into the center often feel trapped and hopeless. "What I saw was vulnerable people trying to make big decisions. I think the bigger story is that when women decide to get an abortion, it's not the first time that 'abortion' has happened in their life." This she knew from hard, personal experience.

Miriam's first "abortion experience" was abandonment by her father when she was only five years old. Her mother was left alone, without any assistance to raise Miriam and her siblings. She still remembers the young priest in their parish telling her that they were all going to hell as a result, but still her mother managed to bring her children to Mass every Sunday. To this day, Miriam remembers her first communion vividly, the lines of boys and girls, "the girls in their long white dresses, and when I went to receive the host it was like there was nobody else in the church. It was such a turning point in my life because I loved Jesus." Though she would have plenty of reason to be angry with her mother, Miriam is grateful for her mother's commitment to do whatever she could to keep her children in Catholic schools and receiving the sacraments.

"There were rhythms of the church and the ritual that stabilized me in a very tumultuous life," she said. "There was something in Mom, and even though I couldn't identify it when I was angry at her, she was solid to that faith. It was something we held on to."

And something that held on to her. Miriam had been claimed by the Lord, and she wasn't going to be given up without a fight.

Not long after her parents' divorce, however, there began more
than a decade of physical and sexual abuse at the hands of her step-
father and an uncle. With this formation—abandonment, abuse, and
a struggling faith—Miriam entered the working world. As a young
woman living in New York City, she found herself in troubled relationships and pregnant, with a partner who was uninterested in helping her raise the child.

"That hurt me," she said, "and he led me to Planned Parenthood."

Even after more than thirty years, the event was still terrible to
recall. "It was a very dark experience and I just remember saying, 'I
don't want it.' I never connected with the thought that I was having a
baby. I dissociated from that."

She was twenty-two. After the abortion, she felt destroyed. She
returned to the abusive relationship only to end up pregnant again
nine months later. "The pattern was set," she said. "He took me to
Planned Parenthood again."

The next years were filled with depressive episodes, a suicide
attempt, and more abuse.

"I used to go to St. Patrick's Cathedral and I'd sit in the back and
watch the Mass," she recalled. The little girl who had once felt the
Eucharistic presence of Jesus so intimately could no longer receive
communion. "That just broke my heart," she said, "and I'd leave
crying."

But something makes you think, hearing her story, that Jesus must
have seen her there in the back of the church, because for no particular reason, one night, everything changed. She awoke in the middle
of the night and sat up abruptly and cried out, "Oh, God!"

"That was all I could say," she said, but that prayer was enough.
Within six weeks, she broke off the relationship, quit her job, and
moved back to the Midwest, where she was quickly drawn into the

Catholic Charismatic Renewal and reconciled fully with the Catholic Church.

"It was a great time of restoration at some level," she said. "To believe that God loved me, that I was acceptable, and I was forgiven."

She met her future husband in those circles. "We were like brother and sister for so long and it was a very sweet, sweet time. When he asked me to marry him, I was thrilled because I really did want to have children," she said. "Once I felt loved, [having children] just seemed so natural. I didn't know how those abortions would play out in my relationship with [my husband] and being a mom, but that experience and pain were there. And I just pushed them down."

That tactic didn't work for long. When her first child, Rosie, was born, Miriam fell apart.

"Once I held her," she recalled, "then it hit me, what I had done. As much as I wanted this baby, I was so frightened of being a mom and being alone with the baby. I wish I had known the Blessed Mother at that time because my own mother was estranged from me, and I didn't have anyone to go to."

But that would change for her as well.

Bed Rest with the Blessed Mother

Over time, Miriam was introduced to the Montessori method, something she credits with helping her become more confident as a mother.

"It was all about observation and letting children try things. Where my bringing up was so strict and . . . with no father living there, that deprivation, I didn't know what it meant to play, but [through Montessori] I really got to see something new. . . . I learned something about parenting. So the children I had after that had more opportunity to express themselves. I would say that I delighted more in being a mom."

Nineteen weeks into pregnancy with her fifth child, Joseph, Miriam's water broke. If she moved or stood up, the amniotic fluid would drain out of her. But if she lay absolutely flat, the fluid around the baby could regenerate enough each day that the baby could grow. So for three solid months, she lay in bed. She couldn't leave her room or join her family for meals. Her children could not come visit her. She was bathed and fed in bed by family and close friends. And for the most part, she remained silent.

"TV would agitate me," she recalled, "and I couldn't see downstairs or the street level. All I could see was the sky and the trees through the window. And that's where I lay for three months, day in and day out. It felt as if I was on the Lord's psychological couch."

Someone from her parish brought her a three-foot statue of Mary and set it up in her bedroom. "I could just turn and look at it and I would be comforted by it," she remembered. "I didn't pray the rosary or anything like that, but I just felt that the Blessed Mother was there. It was an amazing grace because I'm such an extrovert, to be quiet that long, to lie there day in and day out. But the longing to be a mother became so powerful and I think the fact that I was sacrificing for this child, something deep was happening. I didn't feel that God was punishing me, but I had this reassurance that *this* is who I really am; those abortions weren't who I really was. I could lie here day after day and love this child with no guarantee that he would live. And my whole family made a sacrifice for this life, so that's probably the greatest pro-life thing I ever did—being in bed for three months."

On the day Joseph was born, Miriam and her husband, surrounded by their children and a few close friends and relatives, had him baptized. Miriam made sure each of her children also got to hold Joseph, and she watched in inexplicable joy as Joseph was tenderly passed from child to child.

"It was like heaven," said Miriam. "It was outside of time, space. It was this child, handing him over to God. In that moment, I felt a joy like I had never known." Moments later, Joseph died in her arms.

Some years would pass, and Miriam would find herself pregnant one last time, having grown a good deal as a mother. When her last son was born, she was able to give herself to him in ways she hadn't been able to for the others.

"It began at bedtime. I would read to him. But not five, ten, or fifteen minutes but half an hour at least, and I'd lie down with him and read and there was something in that sacrifice. Because when you're tired, it's the last thing you want to do. [I learned that] every act of my surrendering to the tasks of love opens the door to grace for both of us. Sometimes my body goes to great lengths to serve a child, as with Joseph, even to the extreme, but it does not give me rights to their future."

"There is always suffering when you love, whether it's your children or others. Yet those are the very things that strengthen my relationship with the Lord, because I'm not in control. It's probably the biggest thing that has taken me the longest to learn."

Someone had showed her a picture of the Madonna nursing the baby Jesus, and at first she was repulsed; she'd never seen a painting exposing Mary in that way before.

"But all of a sudden there was a connection that took me to a deeper level. That wasn't shameful to see that picture; that was the reality. She cared for him in all those ways, and so did I for my children. And even though I used to gag when I changed poopy diapers (and we did cloth diapers so it was a little more intense), I remember just taking a breath and going back in to finish. That ability to keep going into what's dirty or smelly or difficult, to go beyond yourself to do what needs to be done."

"In living the ordinary life of bearing and raising children, I came to understand that my flesh and blood were needed, whether or not I wanted to give them, and that surrender brought courage and loyalty alive. . . . There was something in it that when I was nursing, it was a feeling of surrender that was holy."

The Fullness of Forgiveness

After more than thirty years, Miriam found healing from the abortions.

A colleague had hung a picture of Our Lady of Guadalupe in their offices, and although Miriam didn't know the story behind the image, she found herself drawn to it, sometimes sitting beneath the image praying. Months later she would learn about the children being sacrificed earlier in the same location where the Blessed Mother appeared.

"That piece just shook me," Miriam said. "That she would go into such evil, she wasn't afraid of it. That thought started stirring something up in me. Who was this woman who could do that and still love, and she didn't run away from it? I think there's a lot of running away when you are post-abortive."

In the midst of these reflections, Miriam decided that, even though she had experienced forgiveness for the abortions, she needed to go deeper. She would attend a retreat for women who had had an abortion.

"The process was gradual," she remembered, "because you're coming to an honesty that you can't anywhere else. But you're with other people who have done the same thing, and there's something about that group community that forms, and then coming to Christ because I lived all those years in Christian community and I knew in my head so much. But here in this brokenness is when I really started to come alive."

She described the Lazarus exercise, where retreatants are invited to wrap up whatever part of their body had been wounded from the abortion. A priest and prayer partner would then go from woman to woman to intercede. When the priest approached Miriam, he asked, "Who do you say that I am?" echoing Jesus' question to the disciples.

"When he walked towards me, I just started weeping and I said, 'You are the Christ, the Son of the living God, have mercy on me.' And I was just raised up out of that tomb and I kissed his hands, and the joy . . . that's when I knew I was forgiven."

That night each retreatant was given one baby doll for each of the children she may have aborted along with one to represent the retreatant if needed. There was a terrible blizzard, and the building where the retreat was held had loose windows through which the wind would roar unrelentingly. But Miriam didn't hear it. She put her "babies" against her neck and pulled up the covers.

"I was claiming my babies," she said, "but I was also claiming myself, and I did not hear the storm, and I slept like a baby that night. That's the first time I had been free from 1972 to 2005. . . . Everyone says, you just need to confess those abortions, but it's not the same as grieving and feeling the pain. You have to go there, you can't [be free] of it until you do."

A few years later, she went on a retreat for survivors of sexual abuse and experienced even more healing.

"As a mother," she said, "you have to go to the root of the pain, and there's a certain self-aggrandizement that comes with being a woman who performs as a mother. But the true gift of motherhood comes in humility, when you say, 'My sin caused this pain for [my children].' . . . I learned that I couldn't have any agenda as a mother if I really want to have a relationship with my children. I have to set my whole self aside. Even as we're talking, I'm thinking about going back to that place when I nursed them, because there was something in that, I was totally surrendered. I was giving them milk, I might have been singing . . . that's what I need to return to, not tell them what I know . . . but speak out of my own lack and what God has shown me, and that just means a whole lot more to them."

Work at the crisis pregnancy center tests Miriam's mothering agenda constantly. Some women come into the center only hoping to determine who the father of their child is. If "father A," they will keep the child; if "father B," they will abort. She says it is a constant process of letting go of control and continually asking the Lord's help.

The center in which she works has adopted a style of life coaching that she regards as the best template for practicing unconditional love. "You have to show up without an agenda. We always start by identifying their values. They have to circle five [from a list on a sheet] and that's how the conversation starts out. We can ask, "If you have an abortion, can you show me how that identifies with your values?" We're really making a space for them to talk out loud about things they haven't talked about before.

"I think that's why such powerful work happens there. They start to get in touch with the fact that they matter. And if they matter, then what do they really want, where do they want to go? A lot of people write off life coaching, but to me it's been very helpful to the pro-life movement."

And, like the healing she experienced from abortion and abuse, this method of life coaching seems to offer an entryway into some of the pain in her clients' lives, core beliefs that lead them to say, "I am unlovable. No one wants me. I don't matter." Her work at the center becomes an opportunity to challenge such beliefs, and Miriam reports seeing on numerous occasions a shift from darkness to light.

"We do believe that about everyone who comes in—that they matter," she said. "Not everyone who wants an abortion is going to change her mind. But the ones who do—all of a sudden they are creating a path forward. And that's the goal of mothering, too, helping our kids create a path for themselves. Even as sisters in Christ, how can we support one another on the path forward?"

It reminds her of the tack she takes with her own children. "I want them to know that they are loved and that I'm going to be here. I'm not going to take care of everything, but I'm going to be here."

"For all the ins and outs of my own suffering and failures and insecurities, I do realize that motherhood was one of the greatest gifts God could give me. Being an unwanted child, all the years of agony and in my own sin and choices, it really was becoming a mother that was the place that I could begin to recover. . . . God has given me so much that it's more than I could have imagined, and I know that who I am today—the whole package, the wounds, the recovery, the gifts—when I come to the Blessed Mother and I ask her to hold me, that's the embrace of heaven. It fulfills things in a way that nothing else could. In her arms, I can forgive my own mother and I can forgive myself because Mary's purity washes [the unforgiveness] away.

"You're right in saying the whole world needs remothering, but in *her* way not so much as in our way. The gentleness, the patience, the wisdom—anything I have today is because she has embellished it, not because I could make it happen."

But her relationship with the Blessed Mother has also given her an uncanny strength. Miriam is fearless when it comes to examining her choices. She knows that her first child, Rosie, suffered the aftermath of her abortions more than any of her other children. And it took a notable toll on her. There were periods of estrangement, but more recently, she and Miriam have reclaimed their relationship.

Miriam remembered: "Rosie came to me and said, 'I'm going to tell you something that's going to hurt.' She sat on the couch next to me, and she's tall like me, and she threw her legs across my lap and I'm holding her and she said, 'Mama, rock Rosie now?' She used to say that to me when she was eighteen months old. I was running a group home for the mentally handicapped, and I was always busy, and she would tug at my skirt and ask, 'Mama, rock Rosie now?' So she said that to me and I just started sobbing. As I held her in my arms, we were both crying. And I just said, 'You know, Rosie, you were the first fruits after the abortions, and I dissociated from you.' And there was something in the holding and crying and the patting her on the back, it was almost like going into the child who was so tiny and there was a connection at a level that we probably never had before. Because if you can't be honest, if you can't name those things with one another, there's an impasse where you get stuck. It limits the ability to love."

After many years serving in crisis pregnancy work, Miriam has decided to resign from the front lines. She is praying about what's next. Enjoying her grandchildren, spending more time with her husband, perhaps writing.

What a story she will tell.

Christ Encounter

Pray: As you settle into prayer, ask the Holy Spirit to guide your prayer and meditation.

Through the intercession of Mother Mary, pray with Lamentations 3:22–23, one of Miriam's favorite passages.

Suggestions for meditation:

- Can you remember a time when God was especially compassionate with you?
- Is there a situation in which you find it very difficult to trust God's goodness or forgiveness? If so, allow your thoughts and feelings to linger with that situation.
- Can you invite Jesus into this situation?
- What would it mean to give him this situation?
- Converse with him about this.

Write: What movements of heart took place in your prayer? How did you feel at the start and then at the end of your prayer?

Doxology: Give thanks for the prayer you have just experienced.

Christ Encounter

Pray: As you settle into prayer, ask the Holy Spirit to guide your prayer and meditation.

Through the intercession of Mother Mary, pray with Luke 1:46–49, one of Ruth's favorite passages.

Suggestions for meditation:

- When you hear Mary's song, what images or feelings come to mind?
- Can you remember a time when you knew your motherhood was especially a blessing or especially difficult? Allow your mind and emotions to linger with that memory.
- What would you most like to tell Jesus about what it means to you to be a mother?

- What are the prayers of your mother's heart that you would most like to convey?
- Converse with him about this.

Write: What movements of heart took place in your prayer? How did you feel at the start and then at the end of your prayer?

Doxology: Give thanks for the prayer you have just experienced.

Christ Encounter

Pray: As you settle into prayer, ask the Holy Spirit to guide your prayer and meditation.

Through the intercession of St. Elizabeth, pray with your favorite image of the Blessed Mother.

Suggestions for meditation:

- If you had to describe the image to someone, how would you describe it? What strikes you most about the image?
- If the Blessed Mother were to come alive in this image, what would she say to you? What would you talk about?
- What special requests would you make of her?
- How does she respond to your petitions?

Write: What movements of heart took place in your prayer? How did you feel at the start and then at the end of your prayer?

Doxology: Give thanks for the prayer you have just experienced.

Questions for Small-Group Discussion

- How has your experience of motherhood, whether natural or spiritual, developed your relationship with Christ? And with the Blessed Mother?
- What have been the greatest challenges in your motherhood? What are the greatest gifts?

4

WOMAN WITH A WOUND

"If I only touch his cloak, I will be made well."
—Matthew 9:21

This was not an isolation of her own choosing. Rather, it was a burning isolation, a filthy sequestration that followed her everywhere: unclean, impure. Twelve years.

Twelve years of physicians and hoping and wishing for just one normal day, one day to walk through the streets and be among her people. One day of living among her friends and family without their fear, their scorn, their wincing at the thought of her approach. *Disgusting woman.* So many years without a simple, tender touch, all affection withdrawn for the sin everyone assumed was issued in her blood. Her skin ached with longing for something so ordinary and human.

On warm days, she found solace near the sea. The breeze off the lake brought a lifting sensation; it washed away the stain and the foul feeling, and for a moment she felt almost free. So she loved to walk along the shore. Looking out over the water, she would imagine meeting the Messiah.

She'd heard the stories, and she knew about the growing speculation. There was something different about this Nazarene, they said. Other healers roamed the region, making grand gestures and promises; she had visited them all. There was no remedy left untried, no physician left unpaid. She would walk along the shore and wait, and dare to hope that the healer from Nazareth might pass this way. Twelve years' disappointment had taught her an uncommon restraint, but still she wondered. She sang the holy words in her heart: *Hear the voice of my supplication as I cry to you for help, as I lift up my hands toward your most holy sanctuary.*[8]

And then, one day, a crowd approached.

Is he there? she wondered. *Is he among them?* She strained to catch a glimpse. The crowd pressed in. Her body shuddered; her body knew first. Somehow there was, close by, a radical new power.

If I just see him, she thought, *I will know. He will be beautiful,* she told herself. And as the crowd drew nearer, she felt something like hope pulling her forward. She would do whatever it took, even with the crowds. She would risk one last time, risk hoping, risk the chastisement for moving so close to them, to him. She got down low and crawled on hands and knees, like a dog, through the throng. She reached and reached, her fingers daring for the touch of cloth, a tassel, *his* cloak. She was stepped on, shoved into the dirt.

Suddenly realizing who she was, people around her scoffed and pulled away, just for a moment. She tumbled forward as they gave way, her arm outstretched. *I lift my hands to your most holy sanctuary.* And then, everything stopped. She sat down hard on the ground and withdrew her hand. She touched her face and could feel that her fingers were hot, searing even, but there was no pain. Her hands dropped to her lower belly and she looked down on her body, this body that had isolated her for so long. She could feel it: the bleeding had stopped. For good. Twelve years' relief poured through her limbs.

Then he stopped and turned around. "Who touched me?" he asked. The crowd buzzed with excitement and concern. They looked at one another, some accusing, some confused.

"Someone touched me," he said. "Power has gone out from me."

When the woman saw that she could not remain hidden, she came trembling; and falling down before him, she declared in the presence of all the people why she had touched him, and how she had been immediately healed.

He reached down and took her hand. The strength and warmth and living energy of his touch startled her. He drew her up to her feet and said, "Daughter, your faith has made you well; go in peace."[9] What did he say? *Daughter.*

The women came to her first, surrounding her, holding her up, looking into her eyes, wiping the tears from her face. Later, they would help her bathe; they would wash her hair, dress her in clean, fresh garments, and feed her, with their own hands begging her forgiveness. At eventide, she would fall asleep in the lap of one of the elder women who stroked her hair and hummed one of the sacred hymns over her, and she would sleep the sleep of a much-loved child.

⟡

When Jesus comes, healing happens. When Jesus enters the scene, the lame walk, the blind see, hearts are challenged, and people are healed. In body, in mind, in heart: Jesus heals.

He healed the sick and the suffering in many ways: sometimes by touch, sometimes by praying over them; sometimes he put mud in their eyes. Sometimes he healed people from a great distance, and other times he healed people not because of their own prayer but on behalf of the prayer of another. Sometimes he healed instantly, and sometimes over time. Sometimes the recipients of healing nagged Jesus, and sometimes they barely asked at all but their faith was so strong, that was all that was needed—Jesus would be moved by strong, humble faith. Most often, Jesus would heal simply by telling the truth—about who we are, about our sin, about himself.

This same Jesus is intensely interested in entering the scene of your life and healing you. Do you believe it? Do you believe that Jesus wants to make you well and free? What might you be willing to risk to receive the healing of his choice? Is there anything standing in your way?

Healing Fear

It started with a sharp pain deep in my eye and a sense of something not quite right, as if a thin film stretched over my eye. I kept blinking and blinking, and the sensation just wouldn't go away. Touching my closed eyelid was excruciating.

I called the nurse at the urgent care facility.

"Don't mess with your vision," she said. She insisted I hurry to the emergency room. I thought this was serious overkill, but I went anyway. I spent four hours waiting to be seen only to have the ER doctor accidentally lodge a bit of tongue depressor under my left lid. He didn't have proper instruments to examine the eye, he said. What he did have told him there was nothing wrong with my outer eye. "It might be a problem further back," he said, looking at the floor, "in the brain." I took a deep breath and tried not to imagine the worst.

The next day I got an appointment with an eye doctor who looked to be about twelve minutes old. He removed the bit of tongue depressor from my lid and diagnosed me with overactive tear ducts. He sent me home with eye drops and told me I needed to wash my eyelids and eyelashes with baby shampoo three times a day. Blepharitis, it's called. I was relieved to have such an unattractive-sounding condition resolved by baby shampoo.

But after several days of dutifully washing my eyes, the only thing to improve was the now-baby-shampoo scent of my eyelashes. My vision continued to deteriorate; it just seemed to be slowly leaking away. Colors became dull, and the center of my eye's vision grew pointillistic, like someone was poking holes in a thin veil held up to darkness. As more and more blackness seeped through, a slow and creeping fear began building in my stomach.

The dangerous thing about WebMD for a slight neurotic is the potential to self-diagnose. But before I even saw another doctor or had another exam, I knew I had optic neuritis—inflammation of the optic nerve—and furthermore, that this was often the first symptom of multiple sclerosis.

The Onset of Agony

A year earlier I had seen a neurologist for a strange, intermittent tingling and numbness in my abdomen and legs. It was slight and didn't last long, but I noticed it more and more, especially after a long bike ride. I thought it might be some kind of sports injury or nerve damage, but the doctor ordered an MRI of my brain.

They found a few small lesions. "Nothing to worry about," he said. Most people my age had a few spots on their brain, and these looked nothing like MS lesions. They weren't the right shape or size, or located in the right place. Overall, I was told that my brain was "rather unimpressive." I've never been so relieved to be boring. He told me to come back if I developed new or worsening symptoms. I couldn't ignore the fact that this blindness might be a progression.

Within a week, I was back at a different eye doctor's office. I could tell it was serious, as his tone and demeanor became increasingly solemn. He held up a chart that showed the vision loss in my left eye—it was a big black blob. "As you can see," he said quietly, "a fairly severe case of optic neuritis." My heart sank. He wanted me to see a specialist at the University of Minnesota, but it would be four weeks before I could get in. So I called my neurologist, the one so very unimpressed with my brain.

I reminded him of who I was and why I had seen him, and I told him about my optic neuritis diagnosis. I'll never forget his response. "I need to see you," he said. "Can you come in an hour?"

I was teaching that semester, so I canceled my class and drove downtown. (Yes, with one eye. That's not illegal—possibly immoral, but not illegal.) He ordered a battery of tests: MRIs of my brain and my whole spine, blood tests, screenings for Lyme disease and lupus. He ordered a high dose of intravenous steroids to reduce the inflammation on my optic nerve in the hopes of restoring my vision. A nurse would come to my home and administer it for the next three days. There would be a series of badly lit hospital rooms, many needles and nurses—one in particular who was a terrible fearmonger—medical bills that took my breath away, and lots of anxious waiting in ugly waiting rooms.

The steroids had the rare side effect of attacking my hip bone. The pain was excruciating, and nothing took the edge off. I went to my parents' house and lay there with my head in my mom's lap, a grown woman scared to death and in terrible pain, my mind racing to the worst possible scenarios. How would I care for myself? What would become of me?

No matter what the test results, the worst thing I was facing, the thing at the bottom of so many illnesses of mind and body, was fear. Peter Kreeft writes that fear is always about the future: about *what might happen*. And long before my legs would go numb with disease, I was already paralyzed by fear.

A Walk through the Garden

I had a moment of near hysteria of which I'm not proud, and my dearest girlfriend snapped me out of it. She said, "Where's your gratitude? You need to have gratitude all over the place. Thank God for the fear, thank God for illness, thank God for his presence in it, thank him for his plan that you cannot see." She didn't coddle me at all—a testimony to her faithfulness as a true friend.

But why did she exhort me thus? What did gratitude have to do with fear?

The Swiss theologian Hans Urs von Balthasar begins to address this in his treatise *The Christian and Anxiety*. This is not an easy tome. In it, he dissects anxiety from a theological perspective: good anxiety, bad anxiety, Old Testament and New Testament anxiety. It is a dense exercise, but you cannot read it without coming away with a bold, new awareness that "human fear has been completely and definitively conquered by the Cross." And more than that, anxiety, human fear, might even serve God's purposes. Like suffering, maybe fear was not something I needed to run from as quickly as possible. He writes, "Christ redeemed, subdued, and gave meaning to all human fear."[10] *Human fear can have meaning, purpose.* The thought was intriguing, attractive, but I couldn't believe it—not yet.

Part of my crisis was a temporary misplacement of spiritual knowledge: I'd forgotten who God was—Maker of the Universe, Creator of All, loving Father, *my* Father, and I was the apple of his eye. I could trust him. His love is credible, capable. This blindness was no surprise to him.

Furthermore, Jesus was no stranger to human fear. His agony in the garden was not an act, and nothing he suffered went unused, unredeemed. His fear had to have purpose or the Father would not have allowed it. "The anxiety of good men is a process," writes Balthasar, "a passage, an episode between light and light . . . the anxiety of the good has as its meaning and purpose to open them up to God in their cry for mercy; it is the banner of God's grace unfurled over them."[11] Could it be possible that fear was helpful, even a gift? That the very drops of blood Jesus sweat in his agony were somehow the declaration of the Father's presence, the evidence of his spectacular power and poise?

Part of my crisis was also forgetting that life is hard, that it's full of every kind of difficulty and that, as one mentor of mine used to say, sometimes life is scary because sometimes life is scary. Having no fear can be a sign not of strength but of mental ill health, a disordered recklessness toward the value of life. That I was afraid was not necessarily a failing on my part. Panic might be, but surely not fear.

Maybe becoming fearless was not always the proper objective. But rather, I needed a new relationship with fear. Maybe this illness was an opportunity to rehabilitate my fear, to take it by the hand and walk it through Gethsemane with Jesus, where he could teach it how to pray.

Partially blind and totally fearful as I was, I was starting to see the banner of God's grace unfurled above me, Jesus in a new and radical way, staking his claim with joy.

"Put out into the deep"

One hot day in Israel, the group I am traveling with stops for lunch at a restaurant on the Sea of Galilee, not far from the stone erected in commemoration of the healing of the woman with a hemorrhage. Israel is filled with "holy sites" like this, those that memorialize not with archaeology but with intention. We stop at the stone and read the passage. It is fresh in my mind. *If I only touch his garment . . .*

While my group sits under olive trees and breaks bread, I sneak down to the water on a little walking path. The area near the water's edge is heavily wooded, and I find a large tree with a wide trunk and a cluster of thick bushes. I tuck into the brush and quickly change into swimming attire. There is a rocky little beach of sorts, and once I am changed, I leave my backpack and water bottles and shoes and slowly wade out into the water. Long have I dreamt of this moment: taking a dip in the Lake of Gennesaret.

The water is deliciously cool, surprisingly clean, the wind just steady enough to create some heavy waves, but I've always been a strong swimmer and I strike out away from the shore. The waves swell. I don't fight them. I turn belly up and let them carry me where they will. I look up into the clear sky and imagine the apostles in their fishing boats, singing their songs over this same sea as they cast out their nets and brought them back in, long days of heavy but satisfying labor under this same sky.

They say that the Sea of Galilee is prone to dangerous squalls, strong storms that develop quickly, and I wonder if maybe the Lord loved this particular attribute. Storms can be so beautiful, powerful. I wonder if it reminded him of his Father.

I let my limbs go limp and float and wonder about the days ahead. I want—and reasonably so—to be ready when Jesus calls, to have stamina and energy and vigor and creativity to apply to whatever tasks he gives me. But over the past few years, feeling "fabulous" has slipped slowly from my grasp, like watching a glass slip from my fingers and fall in slow motion to the floor. It hasn't yet smashed, it kind of hovers over the ground, but I can envision a time when it might crash, shattering into a thousand tiny pieces.

Having no energy, or at least unpredictable energy, does a few wonderful things for your life, however. You lower the bar on everything: how fabulously you should dress or look, how clean your house should be kept, how well trained your puppies might be, or how well weeded your garden. A thousand "shoulds" fall away, and I take a deep breath of thanksgiving for a newfound and most welcome sense of freedom from my own tyrannizing vanities. What energy I have, I want to apply wisely, meaningfully. It brings to mind the hours I have frittered away mindlessly on petty things, vapid things—like television—and I'm grateful for this greater, clearer desire to love and serve the Lord. I take no moment in his presence, in his service, for granted.

But that's not the only benefit. I see the Gospel in a fresh light. When Jesus calls his first disciples, they've been up all night fishing—fishing in the very sea in which I now float. No doubt they are exhausted for having been awake all night and to no avail, for they caught nothing. All that effort, wasted. Then the Lord comes along and says to Simon, "Put out into the deep and let down your nets for a catch." Simon—and I completely get this about him—retorts that he knows best, because he's been at it all night and caught nothing. "Yet, if you say so, I will let down the nets" (Luke 5:4–5), and of course, you know the rest of the story. Nets so full they nearly sink the boats.

What was important was not that they were well rested, ready to go, had the best boats or the best nets, but that they were obedient, even if reluctantly. The catch was abundant not because they had energy but because Jesus was with them, directing them, and they were following his clear lead, undaunted by their previous experience. They focused not on themselves or their own recent failure but on Jesus. They did as he asked, and then they were successful beyond measure. And curiously, then the success didn't even matter—what mattered was following Jesus, staying close to him. They dropped everything, even this most abundant catch, and followed him.

Jesus wants to take me somewhere deep, too, and he wants to bless me with abundant fruit. His will is not dependent on my readiness. When I'm tired and my experience says, "Are you crazy? You've already tried and failed. That will never work," or when I'm simply too tired to believe otherwise, I think of Simon Peter and his empty nets. Maybe it's not so important that I am rested, or even healthy, or that I believe perfectly. Maybe what's more important is that I'm willing to trust him, to take the action to follow him, to go where he goes because he has asked me to, not because I have the energy for it, not because I have the best boat, and not because I have perfect faith in a perfect outcome.

Some years would pass before I would receive a conclusive diagnosis. It fell on the feast of St. Stephen. I took this immediately as a harbinger of God's faithfulness and care. When I first went blind all those years earlier, my dear friend, Fr. Steven, came and anointed my eyes, with immediate improvement.

When the phone rang on that feast day, I was still in bed. The doctor said simply, "You definitely have MS." We spoke briefly about next steps, and that was that. More than anything I was grateful to finally know, and to know that I had been given several years to grow into this new reality. That was a grace.

That's not to say that I do not still, from time to time, give in to fear—fear of what might happen. Sometimes life is scary because sometimes life is scary, but that's hardly the end of the story. On writing about the Christian virtue of courage, John Wickham, SJ, notes that "human life has dangerous limits. . . . Everyone will at times be called upon to act courageously since serious dangers and losses are inescapable. Hence our real question is, what resources are available to us?"[12]

To even think of the question fills me with a quiet joy. Inside, I share a hidden glance with Jesus, and, oh, how he is smiling.

I have legitimate concerns about energy and health and literally being "able" to do as Jesus asks. It is proper to take what measures I can. But I am thoroughly convinced, more so than whenever I was more well, that what is important is not my qualifications—physical, mental, material—but staying near Jesus. Trusting him, focusing on him—not my body, not my past, not success, not the catch of fish, so to speak—on only him.

I miss feeling well. I miss being fit and trim and strong. But I have such a clear sense that if my life does anything good, if I accomplish anything redeeming, anything of eternal value, it is not by my effort or talent or positivity but by the sheer pleasure of my good and gracious Lord. *Let this cup pass*, indeed, *yet not what I want but what you want* (Matthew 26:39).

Jesus heals in many ways. I know. The healing the Lord is giving me may not be in the strength of my body but in the flourishing of my faith, the increase and overflow of a hope I've never known before—a hope that vanquishes fear and every terror of the night. A hope that gives fear meaning and purpose and that gives me a place to go, a dark and glorious garden through which to walk with the most splendid and mysterious company through that terrible episode from light to light.

Healing Unforgiveness

"Forgiveness lies at the heart of all spirituality," writes Fr. Richard McAlear. "Jesus as Savior is all about the forgiveness of sin. . . . He died on the cross so that sins may be forgiven. This is not a minor, optional issue. This is His identity, the essence of His work, the heart of His ministry. The Gospel is not simply about forgiveness; the Gospel *is* forgiveness."[13]

We think often of the effects of unforgiveness: Resentment can make us ill, physically and mentally, and it can embitter a soul; perhaps most important, unforgiveness is an obstacle to the effectiveness of God's grace. When we give safe harbor to unforgiveness—even when we are justified in feeling the injury—we are giving over the very territory the Lord would occupy with grace and joy.

It can be helpful to consider instead the effects of radical forgiveness. This is one example: This prayer, it is said, was found near the body of a dead child in the Ravensbrück concentration camp during World War II.

O Lord, remember not only men and women of good will, but also those of ill will. But do not remember all the suffering they inflicted on us. Remember the fruits we have born thanks to this suffering: our comradeship, our humility, our courage, our generosity, the greatness of heart which has grown out of this; and when they come to judgment let all the fruits that we have born be their forgiveness.

How breathtaking, we think, *how extraordinary.* But we may be tempted to imagine that this kind of radical forgiveness is simply out of our reach.

Fr. McAlear writes that "the first responsibility of the Christian who has been forgiven by God is to forgive others. What has been received as a gift must be given as a gift. This flow of grace is a spiritual law."[14] Let's not forget how much depends on our ability to receive grace and live as forgiven women, how much fruit can be born from it.

The church in modern times has been blessed with numerous, highly public expressions of radical forgiveness. John Paul sat with the man who attempted to murder him. Their conversation was private, but we can see the photo of John Paul leaning in, listening. We can safely guess that forgiveness was offered in this exchange. Or consider the renowned story of Immaculée Ilibagiza, whose family was murdered during the Rwandan genocide—her brother was killed by someone they both knew. She has stood eye to eye with this man on more than one occasion, offering forgiveness—this man who stood eye to eye with her brother and murdered him with a machete.

These moments were not detached, intellectual operations worked out in abstraction. Instead, these moments of radical forgiveness entered the very intimacy that was so violently betrayed and destroyed and redeemed it in the name of love. They embody the prayer of Christ: "Father, forgive them, they're ignorant, they simply have no idea the evil they have wrought."

I wonder at the possible connection between our inability to conceive of such acts of radical forgiveness in ourselves and our willingness to receive the fullness of forgiveness we are offered and so desperately need. Receiving forgiveness requires a kind of death on my part. It is a thorough acceptance of my sin and the damage it has wrought. It is the flattening of my pride, my vanity. It brings that sin I probably hate the most in myself into the light, where the delusion that says, "At least I'm not as bad as so-and-so" is smashed. It is Peter, the rock, denying Christ and then fleeing the scene. Receiving forgiveness means we must go through this gauntlet, acknowledging the fullness of our failure and the damage we have wrought. Receiving forgiveness fully is dependent on our willingness to live in the reality of our sin.

And it is crucial for healing. You can hardly speak of healing without speaking of forgiveness.

Fr. McAlear was one of my instructors at the school for spiritual directors, and in class one day, he reminded us that everyone in the world knows John 3:16. It is already on your lips: "For God so loved the world that he gave his only Son, so that everyone who believes in him may not perish but may have eternal life." But nobody seems to know John 3:17. I didn't. I had to look it up: "Indeed, God did not send the Son into the world to condemn the world but in order that the world might be saved through him." God is bent on saving us, restoring us, healing us, rescuing us, redeeming us—not condemning, not casting off, not forgetting, not wrecking, not seeking revenge. His whole spiritual posture is one of reaching down to save and heal and make whole again, to restore all that has been lost to us. Fr. McAlear says it this way: "Jesus comes . . . not to condemn the world. He comes to redeem it from its sin and to restore its grace. That indeed is the first healing work of Jesus. . . . Jesus comes to restore humanity to the Father's love by the forgiveness of sin. He reestablishes the friendship with God that existed at the beginning. So the first and most important healing is not a physical one, but a spiritual one."[15]

That cannot be overstated. We cannot draw too much attention to this: Jesus' first and most important healing work was restoring our relationship to the Father; it was the healing of relationship, our most fundamental human attribute: relationality. He is an expert in this work, healing relationships of all kinds. Reconciliation is his specialty: reconciling us to God, to one another, and to ourselves. He is the author and master of all forgiveness.

Whom do you need to forgive? Do you know?

A Knife in the Heart

In the spiritual-direction certification program I went through, in addition to class and communal prayer, we also spent three hours a day in private Ignatian meditation. We meditated with a scene from Christ's life or with a Scripture verse and allowed God to place us in the scene, to place us in the Gospel. As you are meditating with these passages, you are asking for, begging for, a specific grace. To know more deeply the love of the Father, for example, or for the grace of a deeper sense of God's mercy, and so on.

The year Fr. McAlear came to teach on healing prayer, he would lecture every evening for a few hours, and on the final night he would lead a healing service. After sitting with him for a week, by that last day I was convinced of his charism of healing, knew I was deeply in need of it, and wanted to prepare well for the event.

It just so happened that the grace we were praying for that day was a deeper sense of God's mercy. As I entered the first hour of meditation, I prayed for this grace, and I also prayed to know what to ask Fr. McAlear for during the healing service. I had been to healing services before, but I wasn't sure what his would be like. And I had an unusually strong sense that I was to ask Jesus to show me clearly what healing I most needed from him.

The day before I got on the plane to travel to school for training as a spiritual director, I signed divorce papers. I had been on a waiting list for several years to attend this program and in the meantime had gotten married and, a year later, divorced. It was as though a tornado had just swept through my life, and getting on that plane I felt as though my whole world had been destroyed. I didn't know what to make of it. So I arrived at this first training session feeling completely broken and absolutely beyond forgiveness. Whether I ever became a spiritual director was irrelevant at that point; I knew I needed to get away and enter the rigorous weeks of prayer ahead.

In addition to the verses that we were given to pray with, we were also given questions to ask ourselves in prayer to prompt us if we got stuck. One of the questions was "What areas in my life still need mercy?" So I began my meditation just gently probing that question, and I got an immediate response. I recalled very strongly a time, many years before, when a woman with an extraordinary charism in prayer prayed over me. She would often receive words of knowledge, insights into the life of those she prayed with. One of the words that came to her as she placed her hand on my heart was this: "You are harder on yourself than anyone else; it is a knife in your heart and Jesus wants to remove it." And without a single doubt, I knew she was right.

Then her prayer went on, and we never got back to that image of the knife. But I was deeply struck by that word, and for literally years, I would pray about that image and ask Jesus to heal me of this perfectionism and self-loathing, though I hardly knew how that would be possible. For years this went on, praying about this knife in my heart.

Jumping forward nearly a decade, as I sat there in adoration, I imagined the knife in my heart. It was serrated, not smooth; it was entrenched deeply and firmly. I tried to open myself to Jesus coming and removing this knife in my heart, and immediately I was flushed with terror—"It's going to hurt if you pull it out. I'm afraid of the pain of its removal. What if it kills me? There are all these people around here in adoration. It's too scary. I'm not ready!" I panicked. What I had been imagining is that it would be excruciating to remove. That Jesus would hand me a twig and say, "Here, bite down on this; this is going to hurt." I saw him seesawing it out of my chest, as though it were a labor to remove it and took all his strength, and it would leave an even bigger, more jagged wound in my chest. The thought of that was so painful, I felt sick. So I asked the Lord if it would be okay if I brought this to him when I had help at the healing service and wasn't alone. I sensed him saying that, yes, that would be better. I was filled with relief and brought my prayer session to a close.

The next meditation was John 8:2–11. Every woman knows it—in one way or another—by heart:

> Early in the morning he came again to the temple. All the people came to him and he sat down and began to teach them. The scribes and the Pharisees brought a woman who had been caught in adultery; and making her stand before all of them, they said to him, "Teacher, this woman was caught in the very act of committing adultery. Now in the law Moses commanded us to stone such women. Now, what do you say?" They said this to test him, so that they might have some charge to bring against him. Jesus bent down and wrote with his finger on the ground. When they kept on questioning him, he straightened up and said to them, "Let anyone among you who is without sin be the first to throw a stone at her." And once again he bent down and wrote on the ground. When they heard it, they went away, one by one, beginning with the elders; and Jesus was left alone with the woman standing before him. Jesus straightened up and said to her, "Woman, where are they? Has no one condemned you?" She said, "No one, sir." And Jesus said, "Neither do I condemn you. Go your way and from now on do not sin again."

The passage was excruciating. I felt the knife turn.

I was so ashamed of my failed marriage that, as I entered the meditation, I was the woman standing before Jesus, and I began to weep. "I've screwed this up so badly, Lord, I *deserve* to be stoned." Everyone else had gone away, but I was fully prepared to condemn myself. I felt like David sending Uriah the Hittite to the front lines so he could possess Bathsheba. I said to Jesus, "This is bad, bad, bad, a really serious failing on my part as well as that of my ex-husband." I kept asking the Lord over and over, "How could you possibly forgive this? How could you possibly forgive even this, by me, who is called to an even greater accountability because of my writing and my role in ministry? You've given me this place of honor and responsibility, and I've just ruined it."

And I was struck by two things: one, Jesus isn't overwrought. He's not casual, but he's not overcome. He's just very present and he turns me to the words: who is without sin? It becomes a question he wants me to ask myself, "Who is without sin?" I reply, "But this was a really big, bad sin." And he shows me the knife in my heart, that it has two edges: self-hatred or perfectionism, which is a kind of unforgiveness—and pride, vanity. I remember a mentor I had who, when I would stumble onto some new defect in my character or sinful habit, used to say, "Welcome to the human race." This idea isn't new to me, this notion of pride and self-hatred going together, but I have a new sense that when I ask Jesus to remove the knife, both have to come out of my heart—perfectionism and the pride that goes with it, self-loathing and the self-centeredness it feeds on. I left that meditation with a deeper awareness of just what it was that Jesus wanted to heal, and I was desperately afraid of the pain I was sure would accompany its removal.

That evening, we had the healing service. I was in the third row or so of folks, waiting my turn to have Fr. McAlear pray over me, and

I will never forget that moment. The very second he began to pray over the first person in line, the very second, something in his eyes changed. And I knew, one hundred percent, that was Jesus standing there. I nearly fell out of my chair.

"Okay, Lord," I said in my prayer, "you can take the knife out of my heart if you want. Even if it hurts, I'm ready. Take it out. Do whatever you want." By the time I got to Fr. McAlear, I was weeping and he looked at me and kissed my forehead and anointed me with oil and touched my face and looked into my eyes, and it was Jesus. It was Jesus.

Fr. McAlear turned to one of his helpers and said, "Let her cry it out."

So, I went to the Holy Family chapel to cry it out. Curiously, it was always a chapel I had avoided. I was married on the feast of the Holy Family, intentionally, and I always imagined that somehow that would protect my marriage, protect my new family. It only added to my sense of guilt and shame. But suddenly I was attracted to it and went there to cry and to write:

Lord, thank you—that was you in Fr. McAlear's eyes—it was you . . .
When Fr. started praying—the second he looked into that first woman's eyes I felt it—you were there. And I said, "Okay, Lord, you can take the knife out of my heart if you want. Even if it hurts, I'm ready. Take it out." And you looked at me—you kissed my forehead, you anointed me with oil, you touched my face, you looked into my eyes, you. It was you.

In chapel, I sat there crying and knowing that it's you and it is all real, all of it, and I said, "I don't know if you took that knife out of my heart or not—I didn't feel anything—but I know you love me."

And with perfect interior clarity, I heard Jesus say to me: "I didn't take it out; I dissolved it." I saw the knife in my mind's eye instantly dissolving into vapor and disappearing. Poof! Gone. So he didn't have to painfully rip it out of my chest. He found a perfect way to heal me—so much less scary and painful, and I thought, "Now, why didn't I think of that?" And he smiled at me and said, "Because you're not God, my dear."

I still felt a slit of a sore spot there, like it still needed to mend and heal up, but it would heal so much more quickly now that the knife was gone. It would go better now, my healing would come more fully now. I was absolutely certain of it.

The next day, for morning prayer, I sat near a statue of the Sacred Heart of Jesus. I placed my hand on my heart—I swear it felt a little sore or tended to or something. I could almost feel the slit where the knife had been for so, so long. For most of my life. Just then, I looked up and noticed a little slit in the heart of Jesus, just like mine. I realized then that he had not only dissolved the knife, but he had also given me a new heart—the plan is and has always been that he would give me *his* heart.

Jesus always has a way—a better way, a perfect way, a way we cannot conceive of—to bring about our healing. The gentle Good Shepherd longs to carry us, worn out, wasted in sin and sorrow and sickness, to hold us close to his heart, to give us his very heart in exchange for our own. It is his identity, his delight, his very essence to do so.

Jesus wants to heal you. Do you believe it?

Healing Hopelessness

Maybe there's a knife in your heart too. Maybe someone else put it there. Maybe there's a resentment or wound in your heart, and maybe you're afraid that to remove it will be too painful, to heal it would be too impossible, that it is simply beyond the reach of God. And that's okay. You may be struggling to forgive or struggling with hopelessness. Maybe you believe in healing for others but not for you, that forgiving and healing you is simply impossible.

That's okay too. If your hope has vanished, you can borrow mine. It is one of the great, mysterious gifts of being a member of the body of Christ: you can borrow my hope until your own comes back. You can borrow the hope and restoration of the woman with a hemorrhage—for she is surely with Jesus in heaven filled with intercessory grace for just such a woman as you. Reach for it, take the risk, risk hoping, reach for Jesus, at Mass, in adoration, in the sacraments, in your vocation. Stretch out your hand to that holy sanctuary and then let him do as he wishes. I am here reaching for you, with you, and so is all of heaven. Risk it. Reach.

Then one day, sooner than you think, someone will need to borrow your hope, and you will find that, against all odds, against all reason, despite all previous experience, failure, and fear, you have more than enough to spare.

Christ Encounter

Pray: As you settle into prayer, ask the Holy Spirit to guide your prayer and meditation.

Through the intercession of St. John the Apostle, pray with John 8:2–11 ("a woman caught in adultery").

Suggestions for meditation:

- What is Jesus doing in this passage?
- Where are you in the scene?
- Can you invite Jesus into this moment?
- Converse with him about this.

Write: What movements of heart took place in your prayer? What did Jesus do? How did you feel at the start and then at the end of your prayer?

Doxology: Give thanks for the prayer you have just experienced.

Christ Encounter

Pray: As you settle into prayer, ask the Holy Spirit to guide your prayer and meditation.

Through the intercession of the woman with a wound, pray with Matthew 9:20–23 ("If only I touch the hem of his garment").

Suggestions for meditation:

- What is Jesus doing in this passage?
- Where are you in the scene?
- Is there a particular healing you would like to ask for from Jesus?
- When you ask for this grace, what does he say to you?
- Converse with him about this.

Write: What movements of heart took place in your prayer? What did Jesus do? How did you feel at the start and then at the end of your prayer?

Doxology: Give thanks for the prayer you have just experienced.

Christ Encounter

Pray: As you settle into prayer, ask the Holy Spirit to guide your prayer and meditation.

Through the intercession of St. Luke the Apostle, pray with Luke 5:1–11 ("Put out into the deep").

Suggestions for meditation:

- What is Jesus doing in this passage?
- Where are you in the scene?
- What does it mean to you when Jesus says, "Put out into the deep"?
- Converse with him about this.

Write: What movements of heart took place in your prayer? What did Jesus do? How did you feel at the start and then at the end of your prayer?

Doxology: Give thanks for the prayer you have just experienced.

Questions for Small-Group Discussion

- Healing of every type is clearly a priority for Jesus. Is there one example of Christ healing someone in the Gospel that most speaks to you? Why?
- According to Kelly, how are healing and forgiveness related?
- How have you experienced the healing of Jesus in your own life?
- What healing would you most like to ask of Jesus?
- Kelly suggests that suffering and even illness can be a source of grace. How? Do you agree or disagree?

5

WOMAN UNDIVIDED

The soul is kissed by God in its innermost regions. It is a yearning
to give one's self to God's way.
—St. Hildegard of Bingen

It was a radio call-in show. One of my books had been discovered by the hosts, and they scheduled an interview. The topic for the program was living a happy, faithful Catholic life in general, but I knew it was inevitable: they would ask a few questions about being a single Catholic woman as well. I was thirty-eight.

It didn't take long. A professional woman called in, about my age, thirtyish, articulate, intelligent. I could hear it in her voice; she was almost embarrassed by the question, but she wondered, how do I manage the loneliness of being single? My heart just broke for the pain I heard on the other end of the line. I wanted to reach through the phone and take it away.

Girl, I've been there.

When you've experienced real loneliness, you never forget what it feels like. You wouldn't wish it on your worst enemy. And though loneliness visits every state of life—I'll just say it, having lived so long this way myself, maybe I've earned it—I think the loneliness that women experience in the single life, particularly throughout their twenties and thirties, has a uniquely challenging character. It can be an unusually agonizing kind of impermanence.

There is a deep yearning in every woman's heart to be desired, to be discovered and found enchanting, to be sought by a great love. And when I go out to speak about this topic, very often, the overriding concern about living life as a single person is loneliness—especially for the women and the parents of girls, and in particular the kind of loneliness that springs from this very deep place: the longing to be sought after, found, and chosen.

I heard it in that woman's voice, and I heard it in the difficulty of my answer. I knew she wanted consolation, a method for its removal, a book to read, a prayer to pray, something, but I was not able to give her that. Instead I said, loneliness is a gift, an opportunity, and if your heart can still break, thank the Lord: it means your heart is working properly. She hadn't numbed herself with alcohol or shopping or busyness. I knew mine wasn't the answer she wanted. It wasn't the answer I had wanted to discover either. But I am convinced that it is true; loneliness—and the loneliness you might be experiencing right now, as brutal and crushing as it can feel—is a gift.

It is also precisely in this place that Jesus wants to meet you and love you.

Good Women without Good Men

Rome, as it turns out, is not the easiest place to pray. It's loud, dirty, and often congested. You have to work a bit to search out the quiet spots, the places where you can truly enter, hide away from the tourists and taxis, and listen for God's voice.

It was in Rome that I first seriously considered consecration. I was thirty-nine. A spiritual director gave me a copy of the prayers from the Mass used during the consecration of virgins. He asked me to take it with me to adoration, to read it over, especially the responses offered by the consecratee. He asked me to sit and pray along with them before the Blessed Sacrament and see if I could envision myself reciting them, if they seemed to fit. I was not perfectly clear on the answer. The prayer responses did not particularly call to me. At the same time, they were not repugnant by any means. I kept at it and tried to stay open.

But the exercise proved clarifying on at least this one point: God does not want my resignation, the approach that declares, "Well, no man has appeared, so I may as well consecrate myself." No, he wants my undivided fiat, my resounding "Yes!" Hans Urs von Balthasar writes in *The Christian State of Life* that "the time before the choice [of a vocation] is a time of preparation."[16] Perhaps God was still preparing me for something—or for someone. Perhaps my singleness was meant to be a sign of hope and joy. Single people have a powerful opportunity to witness to that "waiting in joyful hope" that every Christian is invited to live. It is a good question to ask yourself when contemplating the single state: do I possess a natural proclivity to witness waiting in joyful hope? I wondered about my own success or failure in this regard. I would continue to pray and to wait for my *yes* to show itself.

Sitting in my spiritual theology class one day—I'd been studying at the Angelicum—my professor noted that during the Middle Ages there was a tremendous flourishing of interest in the interior life, particularly among women. He said, "There were a lot of good women without good men," that war and plague had literally stripped generations of men from the population, and in response to this, there was a natural, increased interest in developing the interior life, a greater concern for conversion, a deeper desire for prayer and spiritual clarity. Women's orders flourished, in part as a response to the loss of marriageable men—the convent was a source of protection and community—and in part as a response to a renewed awareness of just how precious and vulnerable human life was. These women—with the men they might have married buried on battlegrounds or outside infirmaries—turned to God, prayer, and service to find meaning and purpose.

My first thought was: Our time is no different from the Middle Ages. Culture wars and cultural plague have stripped our generation of marriageable partners—men and women, surely. Add to these scourges serial dating, complacence with promiscuity, and widespread breakdown in the family, and you can easily see that there is a great wound in our culture—but also, there is an opportunity.

The response of the women of the Middle Ages, if we are to accept the account offered by my professor, was to turn inward, not in narcissism or self-absorption or some medieval version of self-help, but in prayer, in cultivating the interior life such that their flourishing as persons would be assured—and human flourishing is always dependent upon self-gift.[17] From this period arose women such as Catherine of Siena, Teresa of Ávila, Hildegard of Bingen, Julian of Norwich, and the countless anonymous virgins who filled cloisters with their daily, dutiful, simple lives of prayer and work. Women whose hearts were as ready as any to fall in love. Women who longed as deeply as any to be discovered, pursued, and found delightful. Magnificent women who loved and mothered and made gifts of their lives as sure as any soldier on any battlefield. They turned inward toward heaven with longing and prayed, "Set me as a seal upon your heart" (Song 8:6). In return they heard, "Arise, my love, my fair one, and come away . . . for your voice is sweet and your face is lovely." Such women knew that "I am my beloved's and his desire is for me" (Song 2:10). They had their love affair. It was no less passionate, no less real than the love their married sisters experienced. And that recognition set them to lives of extraordinary service, often hidden, and more effective because of it.

I had to respond in the same way: more prayer, a deeper interiority, a heart willing to serve undividedly and quite possibly in hiding.

And I had to remind myself that God is never surprised. Nothing—no disaster, no cultural plague, no human failing or circumstance—catches him off guard. Rather, his plan rises above the operations of earthly circumstances of plague, corruption, sin, and secularization. This divine plan emerges as an intricate, spectacular design of redemption that dances from God's very fingertips out into the universe. I wonder about all the single women I know and whether God might be inviting this holy army into a fresh kind of service meant for precisely this crippled world, this wounded season of civilization. And not only religious women, but single women who are free to do works that married and even religious women cannot. The church is full to brimming with examples of such women. Meet one of my favorites.

An Ode to Caryll

I was formally introduced to the writing of Caryll Houselander in Rome. A friend had recommended her to me the semester before, but it wasn't until I landed in Italy that I began to read her and became immediately smitten with the unmarried, quirky, mystic poet, artist-convert. Houselander's suffer-no-fools spirituality would never shrink quietly to the back pew, as single women sometimes are tempted to do. A certain distancing from the church is understandable if one feels overlooked—and this is a common sensibility among single women in the church. But for Houselander, it would be a tragic waste of life and love, it would grossly misunderstand what it means to be a member of the Mystical Body of Christ, and it would fall flatly in opposition to the Gospel message.

"Everyone has an absolute obligation to live," Houselander writes, "not merely to exist, not merely to pickle himself in piety like a gherkin in vinegar awaiting the Eternal feast. He must live, that is to say, he must recognize himself as part of the whole. He must realize that, as the world's work and suffering are caused by our common debt to God, there is no one exempt from taking his share of the burden."[18] In fact, the Catholic Church teaches that the laity is so important in leading others to the truth of Christ that "for the most part, the apostolate of the pastors cannot be fully effective without it."[19] John Paul said it this way: "A faith that does not affect a person's culture is a faith 'not fully embraced, not entirely thought out, not faithfully lived.'"[20]

If you are on your own—whether divorced, widowed, abandoned, separated, or never married by choice or circumstance—you have a share of this "full embrace," a share in the world's suffering. Yes, a share in Christ's suffering. But what's equally important is that it is a share in Christ's mission and joy. The single vocation, whether one discerns a call to single life or accepts it with humility and gratitude as a result of life circumstances, is a vital, flexible, and fecund part of Christ's Mystical Body. The title of Luci Swindoll's book captures it well: *Wide My World, Narrow My Bed.*[21]

The Love Song of Christ

Houselander, who was baptized at birth and raised only sporadically in Catholic environments, officially entered the church in 1925, when she was twenty-four. But from the time of her childhood, she consistently experienced a deep draw to the mystical, and on several occasions she had visions of the crucified Christ. As she matured, she found herself turning again and again to the church, drawn, like so many converts, by the liturgy.

The Mass brought her back to the church, and her understanding of the Mass has a particular resonance for the single among us. She believed fervently that the Mass

"expresses every passion, every emotion, every experience of the human heart. It is the song of the whole world . . . [and] also much more: it is the love-song of Christ in man, the voice of the Mystical Body of Christ lifted up to God. All our inarticulate longing and adoration, all our stammered incoherent love, set in tremendous metre of the Liturgy and lifted on the voice of Christ to our Heavenly Father."[22]

In the Mass, Houselander saw a place for everyone, a welcome home for "every experience of the human heart." No one need shrink to the back pew because the unity of the Mystical Body was represented not in a chorus of voices raised but in one voice lifted heavenward. The Eucharist makes it possible for us to become one body, Christ's Mystical Body, and the light of this realization spread through Houselander's life like a ray of sun caught in a prism.

It is interesting that her vital single lay life was lived before Vatican II and nurtured an innate attraction to the most fragile members of society: the poor, the outcast, the mentally disturbed, the children orphaned by war. She recognized and honored their membership in the ecclesia, noting, "We are among and one of, a generation of bereaved, wounded, neurotic, exhausted people."[23] She was intensely concerned with the church as it represented all in the Mystical Body of Christ, and she identified our universal calling as "the Christing of the world." Perhaps because she was single, she was better able to identify with those who often stand alone, those who need help to raise their voice in the great, unifying love song of Christ. This awareness is a unique, often hidden strength that many single women possess and cultivate, whether out of natural inclination or out of necessity in their life circumstances, and it's a great gift to the church and the world. It acts like connective tissue, ensuring that the marginalized of our society are not cut off from the Mystical Body, and it helps unify "the love song of Christ" in the church.

As far as we know, Houselander never discerned a call to single life; in fact, quite the opposite was true. She never abandoned or rejected the idea of romantic love; this was a woman who, in her late teens, successfully drafted love letters for pay! In addition to having once been engaged, we know that Houselander was deeply in love with at least one man, a true-life spy named Sidney Reilly.[24] Houselander was devastated when Reilly married another woman, and again later, when Reilly was executed in Russia. But she did not grow bitter. After Reilly's execution, Houselander wrote a friend: "A few years of grief on earth are nothing compared to being together in eternity in God's presence. Also—and maybe this is more important—because I loved that man, I have loved many other people, animals, and things."[25]

Houselander recognized that not only is the Lord close to the brokenhearted (see Psalm 34:18), but having had his own heart broken and rejected on Calvary, he identifies perfectly with the unique rejection, alienation, and loss that single people sometimes feel. Furthermore, she magnified the fact that loving is always good. Love always begets more love, even if it does not beget matrimony and children. To love is never a waste but a holy and glorious response to heavenly grace. She writes, "I now believe that love, human, personal love, is the root of all that is good, and that it is the greatest grace."[26] In other words, we were designed for love, and we needn't fear its demands.

Although she would never recommend to those called to marriage to toss their hearts away imprudently, her own experience in romantic love teaches us anew that even heartbreak or the disappointment of never finding a spouse can bear fruit when joined to Christ's suffering. It can be rescued from the temptation toward self-pity and bitterness and redeemed into greater and greater love. No love—not unrequited love, not undiscovered love—ever goes to waste if offered as a gift to Jesus. This is an idea that many single women tend to forget, inundated as they are with unhealthy messages about romantic love, as though no other kind of love even existed, or as if romance were the magic cure for the most universal human longing: to know and be known by God.

Such a misconception would have seemed ludicrous to Houselander, and despite never having entered formal discernment around the question of vocation, she did seek the guidance of a priest to help form her daily spiritual disciplines. No doubt, her practice of prayer, her frequent reception of the sacraments, and her fondness for spiritual reading, especially John of the Cross and Teresa of Ávila, helped shape her response to the single life that God gave her. Houselander writes of that time of her life:

> I was lonely, in spite of my good friends, but I knew instinctively that mine was a curious kind of loneliness which could never be ended even by the closest relationship with individuals, but only, in some mysterious way which I could not yet understand, by some kind of communion with all men, everywhere in the world. I was driven by a powerful compulsion even to pursue this loneliness, and precisely because it was in the London streets that I was most aware of it, I often walked about among the crowds for hours. I had gradually ceased to look for Christ in the churches and had begun, though I had not yet realized it, to look for Him in the streets and in the people who thronged them.[27]

Note the curious and instructive turn with her loneliness and heartbreak; instead of running from it, she ran to it. To find her remedy, she fixed her gaze not on her own pain but on others and on Christ, on his church, wandering the streets of London. While she may never have discerned a specific vocational call in terms of marriage, religious, or single life, her spiritual perspicacity was nevertheless precise. "Realization of our oneness in Christ," she writes, "is the only cure for human loneliness."[28]

Susan Muto, who writes compellingly on the subject of single laity, notes: "As witnesses to the art of Christlike loving, we must not reduce singleness to some type of disembodied existence. We love as full-blooded, enfleshed men and women who run the risk of loving as Christ did."[29] This was a risk Houselander was not only willing to take but also to which she very nearly ran like a lovesick drunk, eventually abandoning her deepest heart to the most marginalized, most forgotten members of society, working with children and the mentally disturbed who had been traumatized by the war. So effective did she become in this work that there were those who believed she could simply "love people into health."[30] The arc of her single life was so flexible and so large that it sheltered a whole world of forgotten souls even as she struggled with personal loneliness: "The key to human nature is Christ. He is the pattern in which man was originally made, and by becoming one with him, man can be restored to that pattern and become whole."[31]

He is first and foremost the pattern for everyone, and everyone begins as a single person. It is the one state of life we are all invited to master. We must never forget that Christ is the key to our wholeness, and if we let him, he will not only give us important and satisfying work in the church—just as he did for the once brokenhearted Houselander—but he will also love us into spiritual health, and into heaven.

One Tiny Detail

It may have been some of these early lessons in romantic love that made Caryll Houselander such an effective spiritual guide later in life, particularly following the devastation of World War II. She wrote several highly lauded texts, including a magazine article titled "Children and Creativity," which reflected on her years of using art therapy with orphans.

Her theological view, like so many of that era, including John Paul, was deeply informed by her experience of the war, throughout which she worked tirelessly as a volunteer, even during the London bombings. She writes during this time about loving one's neighbor:

"This is not easy. It calls not only for virile Christianity, but for heroic Christianity. Everything now is on a gigantic scale, evil is so terrific that it almost passes belief, such relentless cruelty, such destruction—what can answer it? Surely not a tepid Christianity, surely not compromise? No, only absolute Christianity, undiluted, heroic, crucified love, which stops at nothing and is ready to give everything, including itself."[32]

She wrote this during wartime, but she might well have been writing of our time, or any time. Evil is certainly terrific in our day too, if not more insidious, sterilized, and subtle. Perhaps the greatest temptation for singles of modern cultures is to live too well, too comfortably, and too much for their own self-improvement. Without the communal demands of religious or family life (or the devastation of a world war), singleness can tempt even a well-intentioned overinvolvement with self. As Muto cautions:

> The corrosive emphasis on self in isolation from others and God makes the single life seem like the final solution of the Me Generation. Its aim becomes to make Glorious Me as perfect as possible: poised, in control of my sexuality, not dependent ultimately on anyone but myself, capable of scheduling every day to suit my desires. It goes without saying how detrimental such attitudes are to the life of the spirit. Unless we silence these narcissistic voices, single life risks destroying the transcendent orientation that gives it its reason for being.[33]

And, in this same vein:

> Only to the degree that one fosters caring relations with others can one dare to risk being single. To make self the centre of the universe is an ever-present danger for single persons. This egocentric posture is the antithesis of what it means to live a harmonious,

spiritual single life. For this reason, singles ought to exemplify what it means to care for others.[34]

The call to single life, whether a temporary or permanent state, has great potential, like all vocations, for spiritual heroism. It demands great virtue and courage and utter dependence on God. Rather than moving us to shrink down in the back pew or spend ourselves *for* ourselves, perhaps our singleness invites us to heroic virtue within the church.

Houselander seemed to understand this intrinsically. She took quite seriously what theologian Yves Congar explains: "Christian freedom is not the freedom of a man without responsibility or of a tourist—we are pilgrims. . . . Ours is the position of one who, delivered from bond-service, is given a new task."[35] He goes on to say that Christians are to "pursue their life of obedience to Christ *in the world*. . . . Jesus does not tell [us] to withdraw from the world . . . he gives [us] a mission to it."[36] How true these words often are for those of us who are on our own in one way or another.

Houselander's life poignantly embodied Congar's notion of Christian freedom.[37] Hers was an "undiluted, heroic, crucified love," which was poured out in her writing, her art, and her healing heart. Still, she was also content in the knowledge that she would never become the *whole* of Christ.

As Jordan Aumann notes, "The greatest of the saints exemplified in their lives one or another aspect of Christ, but never 'the whole Christ.' The total Christ is best manifested, as St. Paul teaches, in the Christ as the holy people of God and the Mystical Body of Christ."[38] This notion would burn through Houselander, who was deeply opposed to any kind of conformity. She believed in the necessity of uniqueness as it represented the beauty, diversity, and vigor of Christ's Mystical Body:

Christ on earth, what we call the Mystical Body, means one great *living* in all spiritual life . . . we, who all have the same life, are made into *one* person in Him . . . in Christ everyone exists, *all* experience is known; He has the qualities of the heroes and of helpless children; but we, each of us alone, are finite, very limited. Though Christ in us is *our* whole life, no one of us can lead *His* whole life in all its aspects. . . . So we actually do live just one tiny detail of His life but, taking us all together united in Him, we make up the Christ on earth, the Mystical Body.[39]

"One tiny detail" at a time, we make up Christ's Mystical Body. And it is the work of the single woman to discover her own tiny detail, the way she will take up the "full embrace" of her faith and bring it as an offering to the doors of the church.

"God asks for extreme courage in love," writes Houselander.[40] She would always land there—on that terrible, wonderful word: "love." "This is the first and last vocation of every Christian, to love, and all other vocations are only a shell in which this vocation, to love, is protected."[41] To love is the vocation of every Christian, and like every Christian, single laity must ask themselves gently yet fearlessly just exactly how their lives as single people are operating to protect it.

Caryll Houselander died of cancer in 1954 at the age of fifty-three, having met, perhaps with more love and verve and courage than most, her "obligation to live."

The Weight of Impermanence

Still, there is the real issue of impermanence for those living in the single state.

Marriage as a sacrament bears, ideally, ultimately, *permanence*. This is why the church requires annulments; it recognizes the sacramental and permanent nature of a valid marriage. The soul of a priest bears an indelible mark, a permanent mark; his ordination is a permanent one. A woman called to religious life takes vows—progressively, but eventually—of permanence. A woman called to consecration consecrates herself not for a period of time but for her lifetime. And then there's me—or maybe you—someone single not by choice necessarily but more by circumstance.

I have wondered: Did I discern correctly? Did I miss my calling? My vocation? Or, is there some opportunity, some hidden gift in this ache of impermanence that God desires to give to me, and to many, many women like me? What might that be? Every vocation calls for a renunciation. What is that for the single person?

If you find yourself single when that hadn't been the hope or the plan, young or old, you might ask, is God calling me to the single state? The first question must be followed by the second: how willing am I to consider this possibility?

I am never entirely surprised by the depth and intensity of the resistance I feel from single women when this question comes up. How fiercely they resist any suggestion that maybe they are meant to be single, that there is deep meaning, contentment, and even fulfillment in the single state. How quick they are to dismiss the possibility that in fact, they may be called to consecrated life, or possibly to serve the Lord as a single person living in the world. How convinced they are that the only reason they have not married by age twenty-five or forty or fifty-five or whatever age has to do only with the scarcity of marriageable men. It could not possibly have to do with any plan God might have that is bigger than their personal, individual vision. It could not possibly be that God is inviting them to some form of single life that would build up the Mystical Body of Christ. Balthasar writes:

Most Christians believe—and are all too frequently strengthened in their belief by the attitude of those around them—that there is, in their case, no possibility of a special call; that, if there were,

God would have made it known to them long ago in a manner that was unmistakable. Strictly speaking, however, one should enter upon the lay state only after one has stood, consciously and in full readiness to comply with God's will, before the either-or of the elective states of life. And one should be aware, in the process, that Christian life in the world is usually more difficult than life under vows.[42]

It bears repeating. "One should enter the lay state only after one has stood, consciously and in full readiness to comply with God's will" should he invite you to consecration or religious life. Furthermore, Christian life for laity in the world is usually more difficult than life under religious vows. It is tempting to want to disbelieve that last bit, to think, "Maybe it would be more difficult for others, but not for me."

Statistically it's probably true that most are called to marriage and parenthood. But I have to wonder how many women have given to this question serious prayer and time in discernment with spiritual guidance. It takes a great deal of courage to ask: *Lord, is this what you desire of me? An undivided heart?* It takes a great deal of spiritual poise to wait upon the Lord for the answer to that question, especially in a culture that so highly values speed and efficiency. Sometimes, the answer isn't so quick or clear.

The first time I ever considered religious life, I was about eleven. I remember precisely where I was standing in my grade school, how the sun was coming through the window outside my fifth-grade classroom at the moment I looked out over the playground and heard just as plainly as if someone in the flesh were standing there with me: *Daughter, thank you, but this [life of a religious] is not what I am asking of you.* And in the simple way that a child does, I smiled and sort of shrugged and thought, *Okay*, and went back about my childhood. As the years went on and that occasional tug would reappear, somehow in prayer, the answer always seemed the same: *Thank you, but this is not what I am asking*. It was always rather uneventful, understated. Nothing grand or romantic. No seas were parted, no bushes set afire. It was instead peaceful; there was an ease of spirit about it. So I continued to pray for a good husband and that I would one day be a good wife, and the years unfolded. School and more school and graduate school and work and writing and singing and writing some more. The desire for marriage remained and grew stronger; my time alone grew longer and felt more protracted.

As I grew older and would occasionally lament to my mother about my languishing on in singleness, she would often remind me that if I'd married and had babies, I wouldn't have written books. Books didn't seem nearly equivalent to babies, of course, but I knew what she meant. And plenty of married women write books, so that didn't exactly hold. If you'd married, she'd say, you wouldn't have been able to travel and live abroad and sing and make albums and you wouldn't have helped nearly the number of people that you have helped. And I knew what she meant, but even with my occasional bouts of wanderlust, I wanted nothing more than to settle down, to stay in one place, to build a life with some*one*. And married women travel. Married women cut albums. She'd say that she admired my life, even envied it in a small and not-so-unhealthy way. She'd sit in my quiet little apartment and feel so at home and wish for a place like it for herself—she who along with my father raised seven children, not a one of us in jail yet. She'd remind me that there were a lot of married women who would give anything for my life. And I would nod in agreement and say "I know" and mean it. I know everything she said to me on the topic is true.

But there was something even more that would come to me at times in those years, especially after I'd left the company of friends and relatives with families and marriages that I deeply admired—and

I'm grateful to say that I know a few. Even after I left the company of religious sisters. Something faint but real would come and visit me as I reentered the singleness of purpose that had become the form of my mind and my life. Walking into my little self-made cloister at the end of the day, I was sometimes met with a small relief, a recognition; it is home for this heart. At least for that time, in an impermanent way, my heart fit a certain kind of undivided form.

Does yours?

It is fair to wonder whether I learned this form over the years, learned it out of necessity, cultivated it out of need and not because I was virtuous, not because I was answering some clear call I heard from God. It is, however, undeniably, the life God allowed. Maybe it didn't matter all that much how it came about, only that it did and that God was using it, forming it, building it, building me, using me, despite me and whatever plans I thought I had for my life.

During a retreat for the Missionaries of Charity, St. Teresa of Kolkata passed a note during Eucharistic Adoration to the priest giving the retreat. It read: *Father, please pray for me. Where is Jesus?* I have seen the note with my own eyes, written with almost a child's handwriting, unsteady across a beaten scrap of paper.[43]

The priest immediately looked over at her and she met his gaze, and then she knelt in adoration. She turned her eyes to the silent Christ of the Holy Eucharist. What a piercing moment that must have been. Of course, now we know so much more of St. Teresa's dark night, the years of spiritual aridity and divine loneliness she encountered. She once wrote, "The darkness is so dark, and the pain is so painful. But I accept whatever He gives and I give whatever He takes."[44] That, my dear ladies, is a woman in love. That is a woman with an undivided heart.

"For love does not inquire how far it *must* go," writes Balthasar, "but how far it *may* go. We do not have to urge love to action, but rather to restrain it."[45]

Are we women willing to fall that much in love? To accept whatever God gives and give whatever God may ask of us? This was the word that came back to me when I was eleven and considered religious life, and again and again as the question came back: *Daughter, thank you but that is not what I am asking of you.* Can you imagine how many times I have returned to that moment and asked, *All right then, what is it? What exactly are you asking of me?*

Maybe the short answer from Jesus is simply this: "Fall in love with *Me*." Fall, ever more, ever deeper, in love with Me. Lose your heart to Me! The Psalmist writes,

> Teach me your way, O LORD,
>   that I may walk in your truth;
> give me an undivided heart
>   to revere your name.[46]

And love you more.

Is our singleness taking us to bitter places, or to better, deeper places? Is it biting and fighting inside us, or is it making women out of us? Is it teaching us to cling greedily to life and to love, to collapse in on ourselves; or to grow up and love better, love more, serve more, give more, all the while never settling for crumbs, always knowing that in just a little while, there awaits a holy feast?

> Majestic sovereign, timeless wisdom,
>   your kindness melts my hard, cold soul.
> Handsome lover, selfless giver,
>   your beauty fills my dull, sad eyes.
> I am yours, you made me.
> I am yours, you called me.

I am yours, you saved me.
I am yours, you loved me.
I will never leave your presence.
Give me death, give me life.
Give me sickness, give me health.
Give me honor, give me shame,
Give me weakness, give me strength.
I will have whatever you give. Amen.

Books and Babies

Let's not forget that singleness, properly ordered, has tremendous opportunities and advantages. Prayer and spiritual reading in the life of a single person—and I know this for an absolute fact from the interviews I have conducted over the past decade—are the grand envy of almost every married mother of small children that I know. A spiritual flexibility that most married and even most religious do not experience in the same way.

Your singleness has a great, communal purpose. And the church needs you to operate in that role. Anne Marie Kidder writes that singleness "is a spiritual gift that cannot stand alone . . . there is no merit whatsoever in being [single] unless it allows the believer to be more effective in the use of other gifts for the benefit of the church."[47] Use this time to get to know yourself and your gifts. All states of life are meant not only for an individual's salvation but also to build up the Mystical Body of Christ. The proof of every vocation is in its spiritual fertility, the "more" that arises when our lives are touched by God's grace. If I am given resources and flexibility, they are gifts to be used to build up the Mystical Body of Christ—not to build a better wardrobe or a better body at the gym or a better house or bigger bank account or even to collect my own spiritual consolations—no, every life is designed to build up other lives. The world has never needed women more, as John Paul would say, to invoke our feminine genius and drag our culture back from the precipice of death and sin on which it teeters ever more perilously. What is your part to play in the rescue? Your tiny Christ detail?

St. Edith Stein lived as a single laywoman for eleven years, working as a professor, before entering religious life. When she said that when a woman enters an environment, she humanizes it, she was speaking not just to married women or mothers or women in religious life. She was speaking to all women. Single women can develop this gift in unique and powerful ways—even in mothering. Think of my beloved Caryll Houselander and the children she literally loved into wellness, not one of them her own. I sit in a friend's house and watch her interact with her daughters and think how sweet and intense that love for your own children must be. But I don't want to become gluttonous about it or fixated on the fact that I do not have children. It's dangerous to take too great a concern for my own happiness in this area. For one thing, it is entirely unnecessary. There are a million children who need affection, love, and real hands-on attention. They are not hard to find. If the thought of not having your own children is bothersome in any way, volunteer at a crisis pregnancy shelter or orphanage. Visit your neighbors with large families and read books, change diapers, play cars, hold and pamper and cuddle, or play catch to your heart's content. There is no lack of opportunity to express this legitimate desire and put it to good work.

"But it's not the same thing," you say. No, it isn't. In some ways, it is vastly better. It calls you to stretch beyond your ideas about what your life might be and entrust it in a new way to Jesus. Jesus came to love not only his own family but to love all, to literally give himself to even the least of these. That you can help to mother a child who is not yours biologically is testimony to how deeply Eucharistic your life is becoming.

The Open Wound

Katie is a delightful thirtysomething professional, articulate and prayerful, and she has a heart for the homeless that is as big as the sky. She comes into my office to talk about feeling unanchored and disconnected from old friends who are now married with children. "It's lonely," she says.

I remember those years. Living as a single person in a culture built for two, a culture addicted to romance, whose very economy feeds on coupledom, I can attest to this challenge. Young married couples starting families are not always aware of the single friends they unwittingly leave behind; and those single friends cannot always imagine just how encompassing and challenging it is to start a family.

I wish I could reassure Katie, tell her that the loneliness lifts. It eases. I haven't been lonely in a long time, not the way Katie is now. In my experience, as years go by, you develop more deeply the charisms—the gifts—you are given, and they are put into greater and more direct service. And this: it is virtually impossible to be lonely if you are actively using your charisms. I could tell Katie all this, but I know that it won't help. Sometimes you just need to be heard and validated precisely where you are without someone trying to fix it or even instill hope.

Sometimes we just want to be known in our sadness.

This is another story I heard, and I'm not sure if it's true, but it seems plausible so I'll repeat it here. The singer-songwriter James Taylor was giving a concert when someone in the audience yelled out, "I love you, James!" And things fell quiet for a moment and he looked up from his guitar and said, "Oh yeah, what makes me sad?" What a curious response. There's a great deal of truth informing that question. What is the measure of loving someone? The definition of love, we say, is when we truly desire another's good. But we cannot truly claim to know someone until we know what causes her or him to suffer. We do not really love someone until we come to know him or her in their suffering and, in this way, take a share in it.

Sometimes we just want to be known in our sadness. The good news is that we are.

I'd been studying St. John of the Cross in Rome. John has given us some of the most beautiful mystical poetry of the church. Poetry is the language of one in love, and it's especially helpful to me when I practice adoration of the Blessed Sacrament, when I want to approach the Lord as one who loves. I often took to adoration a particular poem of St. John's. You will recognize the imagery immediately:

1) A lone young shepherd lived
In pain
Withdrawn from pleasure and contentment,
His thoughts fixed on a shepherd-girl
His heart an open wound with love.
2) He weeps, but not from the wound of love,
There is no pain in such affliction,
Even though the heart is pierced;
He weeps in knowing he'd been forgotten.
3) That one thought: his shining
One
Has forgotten him, is such great pain
That he bows to brutal handling
In a foreign land,
His heart an open wound with love.
4) The shepherd says: I pity the
One
Who draws herself back from my
Love,
And does not seek the joy of my
Presence,
Though my heart is an open wound

With love for her.
5) After a long time he climbed a
Tree,
And spread his shining arms,
And hung by them,
And died,
His heart an open wound with love.[48]

While I sat in adoration one day, this image came to me: Jesus is dying. Only he is dying not on a cross but in a hospital. He calls for me, asks for *me* to come to his bedside. I fly to the hospital and burst into his room and am shocked to find him completely alone, shivering in his bed. The lights in the room are too bright and sterile. It is a room without color or warmth. There are too many sharp edges, and the foul stench of illness and decay has seeped into every corner.

I go gently to his side and take his hand that reaches out for me. He is frail, like a skeleton lying beneath thin, starchy sheets—they are stiff and rough, covering his bones. I hold his hand to my face and kiss it again and again, my tears drenching us both. Our eyes meet, and he is looking at me with so much pain and yet—this is startling—gratitude. Though our conversation is wordless, he communicates to me, "You came. You came." I reply, "Yes, Lord, of course I came! How could I not come? I would do *anything* for you."

Just then, his hand begins to bleed and I feel the touch of sharp metal. Suddenly, it is ripped from mine as he is drawn up, up, and we are not in a hospital anymore, but on Calvary, and the too-bright, sterile light has become a sky sick with darkness and foreboding, hovering, low and heavy. And the bed of sickness and death is no longer a bed but an unforgiving wooden cross whose rough shards slice into his flesh, his bruised body crucified upon it. And those same eyes have not left mine. He is looking at me, begging for relief. I stagger and stammer in my heart at my utter inability to help this one I love.

Then in stillness, it comes. I offer the only thing I can: I stay. I witness and pray and weep and refuse to abandon his gaze, refuse to end the excruciating exchange by closing my eyes.

Even in this stillness, I am stricken. With my suffering Lord looking down at me, it is as though I had been wearing the wrong pair of glasses and someone has finally handed me the correct prescription. Suddenly I am able to look back upon every rejection, every moment of abandonment, every time I was forgotten by those I trusted most, every time I was betrayed and left unloved all these long lonely years—and I see that Jesus was there inviting me to know him in this place. Because whom do you call to your bedside when you are dying and all hope is lost but the one you love the most, the one you long for, the one you know will bring comfort and companionship, the one you trust with the most vulnerable moment of your life—your death?

And all these years of wishing and hoping and trying to outrun or pray away a mountain of loneliness and pain has been transformed into the most precious invitation of my life: to know my beloved in the most vulnerable place a person can be known. To be entrusted with his suffering.

No matter our vocation or situation in life, Jesus invites us into relationship: he invites us to stand with him at the foot of the Cross, to stand in that intimate sanctuary of his loneliness and suffering. Because whom do you invite to your bedside when all hope is lost, but the one you know will bring comfort and consolation?

Is it possible that he is inviting you? Is it possible that whatever loneliness your vocation might bring is really an invitation to share the company of Jesus? He invites us there from time to time, some of us more often than others—for some, such as Caryll Houselander, this loneliness is our one tiny detail. Let's pray for one another and receive this loneliness as a gift, an invitation to keep our beloved company so that we might help heal the wounds of this world.

Christ Encounter

Pray: As you settle into prayer, ask the Holy Spirit to guide your prayer and meditation.

Through the intercession of St. Teresa of Ávila, pray with her "Love Song" on page 108.

Suggestions for meditation:

- What lines are you most attracted to?
- What lines do you find most difficult to say?
- Converse with Jesus about this.

Rewrite "Love Song," revising the lines to reflect your own affections for the Lord.

Write: What movements of heart took place in your prayer? What did Jesus do? How did you feel at the start and then at the end of your prayer?

Doxology: Give thanks for the prayer you have just experienced.

Questions for Small-Group Discussion

- If you are single, do you see this stage of your life as a gift, a burden, or both? Why?
- Can you recall a time of discernment in your life? How did the Lord make clear to you the way ahead?
- Can you recall a time in your life that you were lonely? What did that experience teach you? How did it affect your prayer life?

6

VERONICA

When they look on the one whom they have pierced, they shall
mourn for him.
—Zechariah 12:10

From the archaeological and scriptural record, this is what we think
we know: The night before the Crucifixion, Jesus was imprisoned in
the basement of Caiaphas's palace. In those days, the lowest level of
such a domicile was reserved for the animals. The archaeological dig
that revealed what some believe to be the house of Caiaphas bears
such traditional chambers three levels below the contemporary church
built above it, St. Peter in Gallicantu.

St. Peter in Gallicantu was built by the Assumptionists, a French
order, who completed it in 1932. It sits on the eastern slope of
Mt. Zion and commemorates Peter's denial of Christ—in Latin, *galli
cantu* means "cock's crow." It was in Caiaphas's courtyard that the
cock crowed three times and Christ's prophecy of Peter's betrayal was
fulfilled. The doors to the church bear the scene in a deep bronze
relief: Christ points directly at Peter with one hand, and with the
other hand holds up three fingers, and Peter looks back at Jesus with
one hand on his heart and another raised as if to swear his fidelity. To
enter the church, people must pass through these doors that depict
failure and betrayal and human weakness.

In the dungeon-like place three levels beneath St. Peter's, there is a large hole cut out of the bedrock. It opens to a lower chamber beneath it. It is believed that Christ spent the night suspended through that hole by a rope harness that held him in such a way that his toes could just skim the surface of the ground, but they could not rest enough on the floor to relieve the strain of his own weight. The church contains a large, beautiful mosaic depicting Christ with his hands tied in front of him, his toes just appearing beneath his robe, and a rope harness fixed underneath his armpits—that incredibly sensitive part of human anatomy—such that dangling his full body weight from these ropes would have been incredibly painful. Some think it would have been common practice to assign a servant to stay up all night hitting Jesus and throwing rocks at him so that he could not fall asleep or drift into unconsciousness in such a heinous position. All night he suffered, too, the mental agony of knowing that relief was just out of reach.

Another day during our Holy Land pilgrimage, our group walked past an unassuming little shrub, something like a young locust tree. Our guide suggested that it was this tree that may have provided the thorns for the crown of thorns. The thorns were shaped like fish-hooks, and the idea would be to place the crown on the head and twist, allowing the sharpest part of the thorn to be driven into the flesh; it would then leak poison for several days, causing excruciating pain and a burning itch.

The level of detail and wrecked creativity applied to this cruelty is staggering.

I like to imagine that Veronica—who, according to tradition, wiped the face of Christ with a cloth along the Via Dolorosa—probably knew these details. Living in Jerusalem, she would have been familiar with the Romans' various methods of torture. Crucifixion was meant to be slow, painful, public, and humiliating—it was a sign that you had been stripped of any status whatsoever.

Maybe she had witnessed this kind of grotesque spectacle before—the torture, parading, and crucifixion of those found guilty. Maybe she had wanted to wipe the brow of others suffering in this way. Then that day, when Jesus passed by, she was given the courage to do just as her heart longed to do: to offer what she could, even the most minor reprieve, the tiniest comfort. She was meeting Christ after he'd been beaten, scourged, and crowned with poisonous thorns, after he had spent the night dangling in pain and exhaustion. Weighed down by the Cross and physically depleted by his torture, Jesus could not reach for any help or relief. So Veronica reached for him instead.

I like to think that, as Veronica approached the suffering Christ, she brought with her that unique feminine tenderness that has a way of seeing the other person. As A. G. Sertillanges and others have pointed out so beautifully, "Woman is essentially a consoler. Her outlook upon life leads her to be a helper because, since she herself is the giver of life, she is more conscious than man of its frailty and its needs. She protects what she has given."[49]

John Paul claimed that "it is commonly thought that women are more capable than men of paying attention to another person,"[50] particularly in their suffering. I wonder if the tradition of Veronica developed precisely out of the collective feminine heart of the church that, when faced with pain and need, must act, console, and tend.

Veronica must have had to approach slowly, quietly, in a way that drew no attention to herself. She must have had to focus on Christ, to let the entire melee and spectacle around them fall away so that she could see only him, fix her thoughts only on consoling him. She must have had to bend down low, for Christ was surely not standing erect under the weight of his suffering and the heavy wooden beam. And just at that last moment, maybe she knelt before him. There on the ground, looking up into the ravaged face of the Messiah, she gently applied a fresh cloth to the most precious body and blood.

Tradition tells us that Jesus gave Veronica a gift in return for her brave consolation. He gave himself. But not just any part of himself: he left behind his countenance. She had approached the suffering Christ in reverence and tenderness—*Your face, LORD, do I seek. Do not hide your face from me* (Psalm 27:8–9)—and he looked at her, received her offering, and rewarded her tender reverence not just with the memory of his look but with the look itself.

Looking Mercy in the Eye

As a young art student, I loved to paint the human face. There was no subject more interesting to me, and I was drawn especially to the eyes. Our high school art teacher, Sr. De Lourdes, made us fill pages and pages with eye studies. I was so fond of them that I kept that notebook for years.

I never would have expressed it this way as a young person, but later, when I read Romano Guardini on the subject, it made perfect sense.

> The face of man reflects his inner self; it expresses his personality. . . . Man's face also expresses his faculty of opening himself to others and of establishing *rapport* with others. All these faculties—in a manner which surpasses human understanding—are present in God, and that is why the Scriptures say that "God lets his face shine upon man" or that He "sets his face against" those who disobey him. . . . Before God's face man receives his own true countenance.[51]

The face matters. It recalls our divine origin, and it expresses uniquely our humanness.

When I was nearly fifty, I had a bout with skin cancer. The lesion—which, be warned, looked like absolutely nothing on the surface—turned out to be a bit of an iceberg, small on top and much wider underneath. It was very near my eye. After doctors removed the tumor, there was a large, deep, rather grotesque hole in my face.

If they simply sewed it up, it would have tugged on my eyelid, changing the shape of my eye and causing the eyelid to function poorly. The hole was large enough and in such a delicate location that I was referred to a plastic surgeon. So, off I went. He created what he referred to as a "rhomboid flap," and it left a large scar that looks something like a backward, straight-edged *S* on the side of my face.

Walking around with the black stitches and colorful bruising—think Bride of Frankenstein without the screws—was an education. We don't like to see something "wrong" with someone's face. A leg in a cast or an arm in a sling does not elicit the same kind of reaction as a wound to the face does. An injury to the face seems somehow more like an injury to the whole person.

Of the strangers who inquired, only one was a man. It was the women who leaned in and asked, "What happened?"

When I was at the checkout counter paying for gas, the attendant gasped and said, "What happened to you?" She bent over the counter to inspect the stitches as I turned my face and told her the story. "My mom had that," she said, and as I left she offered, "I hope things all work out for you. You take care of yourself."

While I stood in line at the grocery store, the woman behind me caught sight of my wound and her face curled in sympathy.

"I just have to ask," she said, touching my shoulder in consolation, "what happened?"

I told her the tale in brief, and by the time we were walking to the parking lot, she was telling me that her brother-in-law had just been diagnosed with lung cancer. I felt my face curling back in sympathy.

"I'll say a prayer for your family," I said as we parted ways, and she replied, "Thank you, I'll pray for you too."

There is something about woundedness when respectfully, rightly approached that invites the sharing of more woundedness—and the burden is lifted for everyone.

But mercy of this nature is a delicate business. The desire to comfort must be properly ordered. And while he uses the word "pity," Fr. Gerald Vann certainly means "mercy" when he writes, "We must understand pity aright, as we must understand comfort aright. The pity of Christ, the pity which is this gift of the Spirit, is a redemptive pity, the pity that heals and strengthens and up-builds."[52] And sometimes we carry that redemptive quality in our very countenance.

Maybe my love for painting faces has something to do with what motivated those women to ask about my wound. Maybe because the face is the point of encounter, where we first meet the person we as women tend to see so well. The eye as the lamp of the body draws special attention. Except for the blind, whose senses are often heightened in other ways to experience persons in fullness, the eyes as central to the face do something no other organ can do; they can reflect light, even while taking it in. You can be near a person's body, you can hold someone's hand, but you truly enter his or her person through the eyes. You can see something of yourself being seen and received in another's eyes. This is partly what makes iconography so powerful. Think of Our Mother of God of Tenderness. The young Jesus is gazing at his mother; his cheek rests on hers. But she is gazing out—at you. You are invited to enter into the intimacy of this tender relationship through the eyes of the Virgin Mother.

The eyes have it—a certain extraordinary capacity to convey more than words, to express the fullness of a whole person in one look.

What must that exchange have been like for Veronica? To enter the whole person of the innocent, suffering Jesus when he looked at her? Though he was beaten and bloody, weren't the Lord's eyes still "ten thousand times brighter than the sun; they look upon every aspect of human behavior and see into hidden corners" (Sirach 23:19)? Veronica must have sensed that she was being seen as never before, in that gaze of Christ.

And what a mercy to be seen in this way, in such fullness. We cannot forget that, as Fr. Vann suggests, all acts of mercy are first a receiving. He writes that mercy is "not conferring a gift, but asking to be given one."

"You must have pity for all," he writes, "and the greatest pity for those who have greatest need of it. But humbly, reverently . . . otherwise you will have not pity but the terrifying vulgarity of condescension and all the ugliness of pride."[53]

Compassion on the Loose

Of course, pity and compassion can become corrupted and misapplied.

Many years ago, I faced a tricky decision. It was a difficult situation, many nuances to consider, and I wanted to be sure I was doing the right thing. I sought much counsel and prayed my rosary novenas. I fasted and made extra holy hours, but I still had no peace about the direction I should take.

I decided that a silent retreat was in order. So, I packed up my car and headed to a lovely retreat center out in the country for what was advertised as a women's silent retreat.

It was an Ignatian retreat, and if you've been on one, you know that you essentially pray through the life of Christ: his birth and public ministry, his passion, death, and resurrection. And on the evening we were praying with his crucifixion, we were given the entire night to devote to adoration. It is my favorite devotion, one that speaks better to me than all others, and I was looking forward to sitting in that lovely chapel for as long as it took to simply let the Lord look on me while I cried it all out.

As you may have already guessed, I am a bit of a weeper. I have always thought of tears as an anointing, as cleansing, and they have always come to me easily and often. On my pilgrimage to Medjugorje, I was nicknamed "The Great Flood." At spiritual direction school, they called me "Waterworks." You get the idea.

The priest leading the retreat gave a lovely reflection to start the period of adoration, basically inviting us to take whatever was necessary and to lay it at the foot of the Cross, where Jesus would receive it in great mercy and tenderness. I believed what he said. After some time in quiet prayer, I began to speak to Jesus of this hovering question, the protracted fatigue it was causing while I waited for more information to come in, the weariness in the waiting. I collapsed into his arms like a baby. I could almost hear him saying, "There, there, child," as he patted me on the back. I was filled with relief—and flooded with tears. And though there was no "answer" presented at that time, it didn't really matter. I knew the Lord was seeing me and receiving me completely. It was an intimate moment between us.

And then I heard someone next to me, a few chairs over. Someone was holding out tissues to me. I had tissues, of course—a weeper is rarely without them—but I took one, said thank you, and turned back to my time with Jesus. It wasn't hard to reconnect, and after a few minutes, I began to cry again, again filled with relief. Then I heard some shuffling next to me. The tissue woman had picked up my things—my journal, my Bible, my rosary—and moved them, sliding into the seat next to me where I had placed them.

Leaning in too close, she said, "Do you need a hug?" but it wasn't a question. She threw her arms around me in a big, awkward bear hug, and I sat there, puzzled at this weird interruption, and let her hug me. I didn't know what else to do.

Before too long she pulled back, looked at me intently, and said, "You need to talk to a priest!" She got up with some more shuffling and intense energy, no doubt the whole drama disturbing others who were trying to pray, and went off to find the priest.

Much to my continued relief, the priest leading the retreat was a wise and sensible man. I could hear him faintly shushing tissue woman, something to the effect of, "If she wants to come to me, she will come on her own." And that seemed to put an end to it. As far as I knew, tissue woman never returned to the chapel.

I relaxed once again and, turning to the Eucharist, basically said, "Okay, where were we?" This time it took some effort and time to enter back into prayer. By then, an hour or so had gone by and most of the other retreatants had finished their prayer time and drifted off quietly to their rooms. I took a deep breath, and again, I was flooded with relief, and tears. And while I was by no means loud or flailing myself about, I did get down on my knees and at one point even lay prostrate before the Blessed Sacrament in thanksgiving. And I cried. Occasionally, there would well up a bit of a silent sob, until, behind me . . . I heard someone else crying. A woman.

As I cried, she cried. If I sobbed a bit, she sobbed. If I stopped, she stopped. It was either an incredibly uncanny coincidence that the Lord was taking her through the exact same strains as me, or something else was at work. At one point, distracted now, I got up and returned to my seat, only to see that she had her eyes closed tightly, her brow furrowed, and her hands stretched out toward me in what I assume was prayer.

Can I just say this: this would never, ever happen at a men's retreat.

Now, maybe both of those women knew something I didn't. Maybe their intercession was saving me in some way I could not know. Maybe there was some terrible secret sin in me—though I could not remember murdering anyone and burying them in my backyard. Maybe I should have sought out the priest to speak of my concerns at the time. Of course, there is always something to be confessed, there is always more wise counsel to be received. But from where I sat, their "interventions" did not bring me closer to God but rather took me away from the intimate, consoling prayer I was experiencing as a completely loving and tender gift from the Lord.

Sometimes, we don't know.

In spiritual-direction school, it was not an uncommon beginner's mistake to say to a directee in supervised practice-direction sessions something like "I know how you feel," to which the directors would bellow, "No, you don't! You don't know how they feel!" That is, honor the uniqueness of the soul in front of you. She is sacred ground. Honor the unique journey that the Lord has her on. Honor the Holy Spirit, who knows better than you what he is up to in that precious soul. To shut up and listen was one of the most important lessons I took away from my training; it is a lesson I cannot ever learn enough, or practice too much. This quote from Douglas Steere was included in all our learning materials as a kind of theme song and I read it nearly every day: "To 'listen' another's soul into a condition of disclosure and discovery may be almost the greatest service that any human being ever performs for another."[54] Listening is often more about receiving than it is about giving; and mercy is too.

As it turns out, tissue woman was the mother of ten children. I'm guessing it was pretty hard to turn off that monitoring-your-flock mothering impulse, even for a few days' silence. I have no doubt that her intentions toward me were good. She thought she knew.

I share all this in the time-honored tradition of "If you spot it, you got it." I have been tissue woman and praying weeper. I have offered unsolicited advice, made rash judgments, tried to fix it, foisted my "help" on those who did not request it. I have many times thought—no, been *sure*—I knew, only to discover that I was wrong, way off. The greatest gift of seeking some training as a spiritual director has been learning more concretely where my boundaries begin and end, how deeply I need to respect those of others, how little I know of how the Spirit works in other human beings, and how poorly I listen.

At a time I was particularly tempted to "fix it" for a directee who was struggling enormously, painfully, month after month, I called a mentor. She was a wise, humble woman with a great deal of experience, and I knew I could trust her guidance. She left me a voice mail that I will never erase; I listen to it with some regularity.

She reminded me of the story of Uzzah in 2 Samuel 6. King David was transferring the Ark of the Covenant, and when the oxen carrying the ark stumbled, Uzzah reached up and touched the ark, presumably to steady it. The Lord struck him dead on the spot for this act of irreverence. The ark—that is, the home of the Almighty himself—was not to be touched randomly or by just anyone. It was not to be carted about willy-nilly, and Uzzah, along with King David, would have been entirely familiar with the rules and regulations established by the Lord himself concerning the ark. Maybe Uzzah got lax, careless, forgot just what was in his presence. The seriousness with which God's holiness was to be tended was literally a life-and-death matter.

As my friend reminded me, it is no different with another soul. She said, "You know, that soul in front of you is like that sacred ark; we do not go where only the Lord can go."

It is dangerous business to touch the ark of another person's spirit. It is sacred territory to be hallowed and revered. This is why we must be incredibly humble and cautious about any kind of spiritual direction, any kind of intercessory prayer, any attempts to console or help heal the heart of another.

And every act of compassion, in some mystical way, must be joined to that universal prayer: *Lord, I long to see your face.* Even and especially in the face of another suffering soul, it cannot be separated from the absolute reality that this soul has been created by God, in his image and likeness. We see in this soul the very Holy of Holies.

We must go the way of Veronica: slowly, gently, attentively, and small. And at the most important moment of all, kneeling.

Pityfull

In the Holy Land, we were given the opportunity to visit the cavelike dungeon where Jesus may have spent his last night before the Crucifixion. Some call it "Christ's prison."

We began in St. Peter in Gallicantu, that beautiful French church with its colorful mosaics—one that shows Peter, the "first pope," in ancient papal dress. And then down and down we went, below St. Peter's and then below the remains of the fifth-century Byzantine church, down into the guardroom and finally into the dungeon. When we reached that space just below the hole, where Christ's toes would have just skimmed the floor, we stopped to pray.

There was nothing in this spot but a simple podium with a Bible open to some of the verses of lamentation. A man in our group read a passage as we all imagined what our archaeologist guide had told us may have transpired here. It was a sober but moving moment. Later that afternoon, I sneaked back to that space and got to sit there alone for about thirty minutes. I situated myself directly below the hole and tried to imagine the Lord strung up in it, like an animal set to be butchered, his toes brushing the ground where I sat. I prayed the Rosary of the Holy Wounds and hoped it would bring some small comfort to Jesus: *Eternal Father, I offer you the wounds of our Lord Jesus Christ to heal the wounds of our souls. My Jesus, pardon and mercy through the merit of your holy wounds.*

It was my habit to offer up one decade per wound of Christ, those we know so well: the hands, the feet, the side, the crown of thorns, and the cheek that Judas kissed in betrayal. But for the first time in my life, I had a whole new set of wounds to contemplate and honor, so many I had never imagined before, and a wider understanding of the depth and breadth of physical pain and mental torment Christ encountered throughout his passion. My heart was sickened as I started to pray.

But I was soon struck by an incredibly precise sense that Jesus was not there anymore. He was not trapped in this dungeon of torture. I saw in my mind the resurrected Lord smiling, filled with joy, his countenance shining, holding out his nail-scarred hands over this very place—and he was singing. Something in Aramaic, maybe, but the tone was clear: he was singing a song of praise to the Father.

I cannot help but imagine too, even in my miniscule attempt to offer comfort, that in some mystical way Veronica was in that hymn, the Veronica of tradition and the Veronicas of the world who gather up their courage to do the thing they most long to do: to take care, to offer even the smallest bit of relief and tenderness in the face of radical cruelty. Their works of mercy, perfected and magnified and sent out by Mercy himself, emanated from that golden hymn.

We must not forget that mercy is never a one-way street. As Fr. Vann suggests, "The gentle rain has to fall on the withered soil of the soul of man, and renew it; you have to have pity in order to heal and restore and re-create; and then in your pity you yourself are made whole."[55] Whatever works of mercy we extend are intimately tied to a humble heart first willing to be given the gift of mercy, to first be reflected in the eyes of God.

If John Paul is right and women have an unusually uncanny ability to enter the experience of another person, especially that person's suffering, what an incredibly holy and hallowed charge that is. How mightily we must protect it. How important that we humbly submit it before wise and holy counsel. How seriously we must prepare and steward this gift—first and always on our knees—lest we trample the sacred ground of another soul.

St. Veronica, pray for us. Help us to seek the face of God in everyone we meet. Make us women of true mercy.

Christ Encounter

Pray: As you settle into prayer, ask the Holy Spirit to guide your prayer and meditation.

Through the intercession of St. Veronica, pray with Sirach 23:19 and your favorite image of the Lord.

Suggestions for meditation:

- What attracts you to this image?
- What aspect of Jesus has the artist best captured?
- What does this image tell you about Jesus?
- What does Jesus seem to be saying to you through this image?
- What would you like to say in return?

Write: What movements of heart took place in your prayer? What did Jesus do? How did you feel at the start and then at the end of your prayer?

Doxology: Give thanks for the prayer you have just experienced.

Questions for Small-Group Discussion

- Kelly suggests that pity and compassion must be fed by humility. What does she mean, and why is humility important to acts of compassion?
- Kelly implies that being a skillful listener is important to being a compassionate person. What does she mean? Are you a good listener?

7

"MARTHA, MARTHA" AND MARY

There is need of only one thing.
—Luke 10:42

When I first met Rachel, a quiet, funny, fortysomething woman with a bright smile, she was struggling with serious health issues, including the sometimes sweeping and unpredictable loss of physical energy and mental focus. She had seen numerous doctors and finally received a diagnosis, but the road back to health would be long, require significant lifestyle changes, and her health might not return in full. She had several children under the age of fourteen, one with special educational needs, and a husband who traveled a fair amount for work and often left her on her own to parent and tend the household. With the added burden of managing difficult symptoms, she was teetering on the edge of a debilitating depression. Though she deeply desired it, she struggled to get recollected enough to pray. No big shock there.

In an email to me not long after we began meeting, she wrote about balancing the many demands on her time with an increasing desire for prayer and silence and a special hunger to practice adoration of the Blessed Sacrament. An introvert with a need for stillness and a love for writing, she felt lonely and isolated and often judged by the world around her as inadequate—as a woman, as a wife and mother, and as a homemaker. She described pain in her innermost being and how it was exacerbated by a belittling voice in her head, one that told her she was a failure, chiding, "Why can't you just keep up with the laundry? How hard is that?"

Do you know that voice?

Failure and the Better Part

In a fresh way, Rachel's situation brings to mind the Martha and Mary story of Luke's Gospel (10:38–42). The Lord comes for a visit, and Martha welcomes him into her home. She busies herself with the necessary hospitality of having such a guest, while her sister, Mary, sits at the Lord's feet, listening. The church fathers often parsed out the two women's reactions as one woman embodying the active life, the other woman, the contemplative, and the need to integrate both active and contemplative charisms to live a fruitful Christian life. There was the added implication that time with the Lord must hold a certain primacy because it situates and feeds the active life. Fair enough, we think.

Still, it's Martha who is chastised by the Lord when she points out that she's doing all the work and Mary is *only* listening. "Tell her to help me," she says, and I can understand that. There's real work to do in preparing a nourishing meal, especially if the guests are unexpected. Her request does not seem wildly unreasonable, so we might ask what the Lord is up to in his response.

"Martha, Martha," the Lord replies, calling her by name twice—you can almost see him shaking his head in exasperation—"you are worried and distracted by many things; there is need of only one thing. Mary has chosen the better part, which will not be taken away from her."

Sometimes, when we read the Martha and Mary story, I think we imagine Martha to be a distracted, nitpicking busybody and Mary her recollected, spiritually superior sister. I want to identify with Mary, who humbly sat at the Lord's feet, choosing the better part. I am tempted to judge Martha as shallow and petty. But I wonder if "Martha, Martha" and Mary weren't really more representative of just one woman, maybe a woman a lot like Rachel, perhaps a lot like you: torn between the deep desire to cultivate that contemplative listening ear and the real demand to meet the needs of family, work, and health. For many women, you could add to the list: care for aging parents or a sick spouse or child, volunteer service to the poor or underprivileged, community and parish involvement, grandchildren, and the like.

Is it just a matter of "work-life balance"? Martha needs more "me time," or just needs to get a massage and relax? Is the Lord asking us to slow down and work less? Furthermore, he calls Mary's choice, to be still and listen to the Lord, "the better part." Is he suggesting that the active life is lesser? And how do we appropriate that against the real work of life: caring for families, earning an income and managing our health, forming and educating our children, caring for the poor and marginalized around us?

That hardly fits when we consider the lives of some of our great contemporary saints, St. Teresa of Kolkata or Pope St. John Paul II, for example. Though both their lives were fed by a radical fidelity to prayer even in times of great difficulty or aridity, they may have accomplished more real works of mercy between the two of them than everyone in the Northern Hemisphere combined. They might be deemed "workaholics" by modern standards of psychological fitness.

It's interesting to note, however, that the Lord does not challenge Martha for her hospitality—happily opening her home to him, serving him, nourishing him after his journey; these are great goods and probably expressions of the charisms God has given her. Furthermore, we know that Jesus himself was a laborer; he was no stranger to the demands of real-life work and its divine potential to sanctify. John Paul reminds us that "awareness that *man's work is a participation in*

God's activity ought to permeate . . . even 'the most ordinary every-
day activities. For, while providing the substance of life for themselves
and their families, men and women are performing their activities in
a way which appropriately benefits society. They can justly consider
that by their labour they are unfolding the Creator's work.'"[56] Which
is to say that work is part of how we image God; it is part of how
we participate in his divine life—even the most tedious or tiny works
such as changing a diaper or bedpan, washing the clothes, or making
a meal. And John Paul emphasizes that this truth "was given particular prominence by Jesus Christ."[57] Martha probably felt called to hospitality and experienced sincere Christian joy in extending it. Clearly,
Jesus was not opposed to her good works.

Rather, he challenged her for worry and distraction; at least for
a moment, she lost sight of eternity. She took her internal gaze off
Christ and serving him through this charism of hospitality and shifted
her attention to the listening Mary. It was not Martha's good works
that were a problem. It was the distraction and worry that stole her
focus. Distraction and worry stand in direct opposition to the message of the Gospel, and that is why Jesus wanted, with some special
emphasis, to free Martha from them.

Maybe the Lord is warning all of us against taking up a "Martha,
Martha" approach to the spiritual life. Maybe the Lord tells us,
through Martha's story, to guard against anything that takes us away
from an eternal view: comparisons, judgment, distraction with passing things, worry that is "out of order," particularly the fear of what
others think. The list of distractions and worries we might take up
is endless. Distraction has become a major part of our lifestyle and
economy. Worry and womanhood seem to go hand in hand, thanks
to all the responsibilities that we have taken on and that have been
entrusted to us.

It doesn't help that we live in a very "Martha, Martha" culture—one wildly distracted with the nonessential, invested in comparisons of no value, preoccupied with passing and superficial worries—and we have lived this way for such a long time that "distracted living" is considered normal. Romano Guardini writes of it this way: "Man in this state is not really a person who speaks or who can be spoken to, but merely an uncoordinated bundle of thoughts, feelings, and sensations."[58] We've lost our natural ability to serve in a recollected way and perhaps to recognize the proper time to sit at the feet of all wisdom and listen—and the "proper time" varies in duration and method from one individual to another.

In her excellent book *Quiet: The Power of Introverts in a World That Can't Stop Talking*, Susan Cain argues that extroversion has won out over introversion as the accepted cultural ideal—and this, at least to some degree, to our detriment. The book is full of quotes like this one from Mahatma Gandhi: "In a gentle way, you can shake the world"; and from Einstein, "I am a horse for a single harness, not cut out for tandem or teamwork . . . for well I know that in order to attain any definite goal, it is imperative that one person do the thinking and the commanding." Cain argues that solitude may be an important key to creativity (as opposed to the groupthink methods applied widely in business, research, and especially in our system of early education). If her theory holds, I would extend it to the recollected soul as well. When solitude loses its pride of place in human experience, all human experience suffers.[59]

Certainly extroverts can be well recollected, but I wonder if it isn't introverts who show them the way. Consider, as does Sherry Turkle in another fine work, *Alone Together: Why We Expect More from Technology and Less from Each Other*:

The self shaped in a world of rapid response measures success by calls made, e-mails answered, texts replied to, contacts reached. . . . We insist that our world is increasingly complex, yet we have created a communications culture that has decreased the time available for us to sit and think uninterrupted. As we communicate in ways that ask for almost instantaneous responses, we don't allow sufficient space to consider complicated problems.[60]

The effects of a "connected life" are not restricted to our business practices. They have invaded and overtaken our homes and personal lives and most especially our young people. Turkle cites the disturbing reality that young people feel anxious and unsettled if they are separated from their phones.

Speed and activity conquer all. But cultivating a recollected heart that enters readily into prayer and contemplation of the deepest, most meaningful things is not something we can do quickly or busily. Recollection is not a process of efficiency or even a personal achievement; it is rooted more in emptiness, stillness. It is a hidden gift from God that requires patience, practice, repetition, and, ultimately, humility, the decision to make ourselves available, without an agenda, to the work of the Holy Spirit. To our distracted world, the practice of spiritual recollection might even look like a waste of time. Meekness and interiority are seen as weaknesses to be overcome, even medicated or educated out of us with assertiveness training.

Guardini would argue that distraction is not simply an obstacle to prayer; it's an obstacle to our flourishing as human beings. He claims that "recollectedness is not an isolated condition but the mind's right and proper state, the state which enables man to establish the right relationship to men and things."[61] He explains:

The basic meaning of the word *recollected* is "to be unified, gathered together." A glance at our life will show how much we lack this aptitude. We should have a fixed center which, like the hub of a wheel, governs our movements and from which all our actions go out and to which they return; a standard, also, or a code by

which we distinguish the important from the unimportant, the
end from the means, and which puts actions and experiences into
their proper order; something stable, unaffected by change and
yet capable of development, which make it clear to us who we
are and how matters stand with us. We lack this; we, the men of
today, lack it more than did those who lived in earlier ages.[62]

He was writing in 1957. Can you imagine what he might think about
our distractions now and the speed (and vapidness) with which we
frequently communicate, even in matters of heart and soul?

In light of this, Rachel's depression makes perfect sense. She has
been created to seek these right relationships and this fixed, nuanced
spiritual center, yet the present circumstances of her life have made it
virtually impossible to locate and inhabit it with regularity. The battle to keep eternity in its proper place against the demands of a distracted world—one ready to shame you for not having the right car,
or house, or clothes, or phone, or the most accomplished children,
the most attractive body—is real and formidable. It can take loads of
energy to "come out from among" the cultural squall.

When Jesus calls, "Martha, Martha," I don't think he's shaking his
head at her in exasperation or telling her she simply needs to slow
down or mind her own business. I think he's inviting her to this radical reordering, calling her back to a recollected state, to remind her
who she really is and how even her hospitality must be rooted in and
fed from that listening place. And he's reminding her: *You are in the
presence of the Eucharistic Savior.* When Rachel feels on the verge of
depression because she cannot cultivate this right and proper state, we
want to put her on medication or send her to therapy, not necessarily
address this fundamental, radical challenge to reorder things so that
she can spend time in the presence of Jesus.

Let me be clear: the last thing I want to suggest is that Rachel
is at fault or "not doing it right" because she can't do it all, or

that caring for a large family isn't a high priority, or that caring for her health is a "distraction" or a silly worry. On the contrary, I think her symptoms are probably great evidence that she indeed is ordered properly, and maybe medication and therapy, whether for a time or as an ongoing contribution to her health regimen, would be extremely helpful. Rather, I want to give her—and so many women like her—permission and resounding support to reject the demands of an unrecollected culture driven by distraction and unnecessary worry, so that there is more time to do what Christ is calling her to do: *to be with him.*

You might say I am inviting women to *fail.*

All of Christianity is built upon a "failed" Messiah. Guardini points out that "the abiding figure of Jesus's life is failure, defeat. Humanly speaking, there has never been a great personality, filled with the glories of the Spirit and endowed with grace, who came to such a wretched end as He did. Unless we open ourselves to this fact, the figure of our Lord and His earthly life may appear trivial and idyllic, and its immense majesty will escape us."[63]

It's probably not unreasonable to imagine that Christ was a successful carpenter. Some people may have scoffed when he dropped that worthy enterprise to preach and teach and heal. When he took to the mountains to pray, no doubt he left some people disappointed by the loss of his company, or others may have judged him as selfish for stealing away. Maybe he looked like a loser to those who failed to understand: he wasn't building a business, he was building a kingdom, and what people thought of him was not a consideration. We cannot ignore the fact that, if his is a life of failure, we are called not only to admire it but also to participate in it.

And thus, my invitation. Maybe what those of us who struggle with Martha-like worry and distraction need is a healthy dose of the Lord's failure.

Coming Unplugged

My phone is not a smartphone; it is a very, very dumb phone, a dinosaur. For example, it cannot decipher about 50 percent of the texts that come to me. With more and more folks relying on text messaging for their communications, I occasionally consider upgrading it. But I haven't for a few reasons. One, I hate texting, and so having lesser capacities in that arena is no loss to me. Two, an upgrade would be unnecessarily expensive and those monies are better spent elsewhere. And three, the only operation I use on the phone regularly is the phone itself. My phone doesn't need to do anything else for me and the life I've chosen. I don't use it for spiritual direction or to locate restaurants or to stay connected to my email or to shop online. Its only function for me is as a phone. And that's enough. There's nothing wrong with having a sophisticated phone. A dear girlfriend can, through her phone, track where her teenage girls are—and they can see where she is throughout her workday too—a handy feature for any family. But I can get away with something much simpler.

When folks learn of my "communications strategy," they are sometimes incredulous. One woman who wanted to set appointments with me through "texting" was shocked when I told her I would not schedule appointments that way. She sat up straight in her chair and said, "That's really countercultural." I chuckled and thought, *I'm a relic.* If only she knew.

I don't have television. I rarely go to shopping malls. My food plan is extremely simple, even monotonous. I try to limit my Internet use to a few regular sites: the weather, the bank, a few news sources, the occasional search for Mass times and the like. As I've aged, my wardrobe has become more of a uniform, with fewer options to consider. Time grows short when you get older, and the desire to jettison anything inessential grows with it. I'm confident that on my death bed I won't be thinking, *If only I'd watched more television or spent more time shopping.* Still, I haven't made these choices because I'm virtuous but more the opposite—because I need all the help I can get to maintain a simple, quiet, recollected life. It takes some determination, a decision to withdraw from some aspects of the mainstream.

There are distractions from within and distractions from without; those I can control entirely and those I have to manage. My point is not to shame anyone or her habits of life but to invite you to examine your relationship with those distractions and worries that are clearly in your control and see if there aren't ways to radically simplify things, to even "fail" by cultural standards, and leave a little more room for sitting at the feet of Jesus, listening.

Being quiet before the Lord is not optional, something we squeeze in when we get a free moment—though that can be a great thing to do too. Quiet prayer has to feed the stream of life, the stream of our choices. Quiet must be a priority. For so many women stretched across multiple plains of demand, it requires an act of near heroism to reject whatever passing distraction or thin social pressure might be tugging at their time and go sit at the feet of Jesus in the adoration chapel instead.

St. Edith Stein said that "to have divine love as its inner form, a woman's life must be a Eucharistic life."[64] And in another essay, "It is most important that the Holy Eucharist becomes life's focal point: that the Eucharistic Savior is the center of existence; that every day is received from His hand and laid back therein; that the day's happenings are deliberated with him."[65]

This was the invitation to Martha: to reorder her center of existence on the living Eucharist who came to break bread with her.

The Unquiet Universal Trance

It cannot be overlooked that Jesus in the Blessed Sacrament is—for the majority of us—silent. In this, we are invited to imitate him.

Oddly enough, my journey into the practice of silence began with television.

One Christmas, many years ago, I gave my television away. I had been spending more time in adoration, which made me want to spend only more time in adoration. About the same time, I decided that I wanted a real Christmas. You know how this goes: every holiday season, about the end of November, all the ads begin. Weary of my own life not looking like a credit card commercial, aware that I had the blasted box on far too much anyway, and, finally, desiring to purge these bizarre messages about the meaning of Christmas from my home and my head and heart, I got rid of "the thing."

Two weeks later—following what I confess was a brief period of rather pained withdrawal—I knew I never wanted "the thing" back. A peace had descended upon my house, my writing, and my life that I had not experienced for a long time. Perhaps never. I immediately started publishing again, my thinking became clearer, more vibrant, and even as a working musician, which I was at the time, I began to crave silence. As St. John of the Cross says, "My house being now all stilled."

Over the years, I've had occasional roommates or living situations in which television was reintroduced. There were even times when people learned that I didn't have a television and showed up at my house with a television to donate! I learned that there are "TV apostles." Without fail, I noticed the effect its presence had on my thinking and my prayer life—and still I was drawn to it. For me, having a television in my home was like handing an active alcoholic the keys to a well-stocked liquor store. Now, with the option of streaming programs through the Internet, there are still more ways for television and the culture it purports to have to invade my life. I have to be attentive; it is a constant battle.

It dawned on me that not one of the great thinkers, writers, poets, theologians, artists, or saints—not one mind or soul that I admired and called on for intercession and wisdom—not one had a television or anything like it (or ever went to the mall, by the way). I liked very much what Thomas Merton once wrote about television:

> I have watched TV *twice* in my life. Certainly I do not pretend that by simply refusing to keep up with the latest news I am therefore unaffected by what goes on, or free of it all. . . . Nine tenths of the news, as printed in the papers, is pseudo news, manufactured events. Some days ten tenths. The ritual morning trance, in which one scans columns of newsprint, creates a peculiar form of generalized pseudo attention to a pseudo-reality. This experience is taken seriously, it is one's daily immersion in "reality." . . . My own experience has been that *renunciation* of this self-hypnosis, of this participation in the *unquiet universal trance*, is no sacrifice of reality at all. To "fall behind" in this sense is to get out of the big cloud of dust that everybody is kicking up, to breathe and to see a little more clearly.[66]

This was and has been my experience in turning off the television: to renounce participation in the "unquiet universal trance." And for me, it was necessary to enter the kind of recollection that invites silence and contemplation. This renunciation—in conjunction with the work of silence—is the means to breathe more deeply, to see a little more clearly, and, paradoxically, to hear a little more clearly the silent Christ of the Eucharist.

In Silence, My Soul Waits

You cannot encounter the life of the church without this radical invitation to silence before the Lord. John of the Cross writes, "The Father spoke one word from all eternity and he spoke it in silence, and it is in silence that we hear it." Or consider the Psalms: "For

God alone my soul waits in silence" (62:1). Or Song of Songs, which speaks of "a time to keep silence, and a time to speak" (3:7). Or the Gospel of Mark, when Jesus is speaking to the stormy sea but he is clearly also speaking to stormy me: "Peace! Be still!" (4:39). Nearly all the prophets summon us to silence: "The Lord is in his holy temple; let all the earth keep silence before him!" (Habakkuk 2:20). I could go on and on.

Why? Because silence speaks to the character of God, the essence and nature of God, in a way that words, songs, and writing do not. It creates room for awe, which the church teaches us is really the only appropriate response to a real encounter with God.

But this silence, again, is not simply an hour spent here or there in adoration—though that's a good thing to do: it is more of a posture to be drawn into all of life, the recollected heart that Guardini speaks of fostering. Ridding my home of the television was only the start. Other pointless distractions started to fall away as well—most notably and helpfully, shopping. I left the radio off in the car and spent more time sitting quietly in the tabernacle at church—without an agenda. I learned, as Merton noted, that "the silence of the sacristy has its own sound." I started to attend silent retreat weekends and enjoyed immensely the spiritual practice of silence in the company of others. When your silence is ordered well, you can grow incredibly close to others without saying a word. Silence can be a powerful mystical tool for building community, one the church needs a great deal, I think.

As a younger person, I had sometimes complained, "God, why won't you answer me? Why won't you talk to me?" In practicing silence, I realized that the still small voice of God was always there, but I had been unwilling and unable to listen. I had not quieted myself enough to listen because I couldn't remember what silence sounded like, and I confess I was probably deeply in love with and attached to my own words. We are a culture addicted to talking and to our own opinions. We firmly believe, particularly as Americans, that our opinions are absolutely invaluable to the universe. We must, at every opportunity, espouse our opinions quickly, loudly, and broadly, however uneducated or reactionary they may be. But as St. Francis of Assisi reminds us (this phrase is often attributed to him), we are to "preach often and, when necessary, use words." That posture—to preach often in our actions, not in our words—requires a certain kind of interiority, which is cultivated in part in the spiritual discipline of silence and its intrinsic relationship to listening. It is, in short, sitting at the feet of the Eucharistic Savior, listening.

Maybe television is not an issue in your home. Maybe there are other forms of empty distraction or useless worry that are obstacles to your spiritual life. Given that we live in a culture that has built distraction into our very economy, it can be helpful to ask these questions in our daily prayer of review, our Examen: Does my life regularly include silence, the prayer of quiet? Are there distractions I could put away? Worries I could leave at the tabernacle? Silence before the Lord is a great act of love and trust. It disciplines the heart. Silence assumes that what I have to say is never going to be more important than what God has to say to me. As the desert father Ammonas has written, "I have shown you the power of silence, how thoroughly it heals and how fully pleasing it is to God. . . . Know that it is by silence that the saints grew, that it was because of silence that the power of God dwelt in them, because of silence that the mysteries of God were known to them."[67]

The prayer of silence, the prayer of quiet, is also a protective measure. We find privacy in silence. It restores us to a holy privacy, the protectiveness of all that is most sacred to the human person and necessary to our flourishing and so very lost in our culture of "reality television," people openly weeping on talk shows about the most intimate parts of their lives as though doing so were a good thing. Silence restores us to a proper sense, not of confessional living—telling every-body everything—but of confessed living and proper repentance.

Is this just another way to say that we should all become contem-platives? Well, to a degree, yes. But perhaps not contemplatives in the way that we think we understand the title, but more in the mode of Mary sitting at Christ's feet, listening. More in the way of choosing the better part throughout the day, in the smallest things, in the hid-denness of the heart where only a silent Christ bears witness.

"Rachel, Rachel"

What do you think the Lord would say to Rachel? "You are worried and distracted about many things. Choose the better part"?

I'm not going to tell you how things began to unfold for Rachel. In part, because her story is still unfolding—maybe I'll have an update soon—and in part because it's less important to know the details of her story than to discern what Jesus would say to you.

Take that to prayer, pose it to the silent Christ of the Eucharist, and let me know what you discover. I wish you the best in this exer-cise: a healthy dose of failure.

Christ Encounter

Pray: As you settle into prayer, ask the Holy Spirit to guide your prayer and meditation.

Through the intercession of St. Martha, pray with Luke 10:38–42.

Suggestions for meditation:

- Where do you see yourself in this scene?
- What are you doing?
- How does Jesus address you?
- What would you like to say in return?

Write: What movements of heart took place in your prayer? What did Jesus do? How did you feel at the start and then at the end of your prayer?

Doxology: Give thanks for the prayer you have just experienced.

Questions for Small-Group Discussion

- In what ways was Jesus a "failure"? What does Kelly mean when she encourages us to "fail"?
- Do an evaluation of your daily or weekly quiet time. Do you think you get enough prayer time? How might you invite greater recollection or quiet reflection into your daily life?

8

QUEEN

A great portent appeared in heaven: a woman clothed with the
sun, with the moon under her feet, and on her head a crown of
twelve stars.

—Revelation 12:1

That pivotal moment was always with her. The memory came often
to her mind, washing over her while she said her prayers or sang the
holy songs, made the bread, mended the clothes, or when she first
opened her eyes upon the day.

Mostly the memory would visit as she was drifting into sleep.
With the evening prayers still humming in her breast—*Sh'ma Yisra'eil*
Adonai Eloheinu Adonai echad. Hear, O Israel, the Lord is our God,
the Lord is one—she would close her eyes. But sometimes, instead
of darkness, there was light, such a beautiful, inviting light, and she
could feel it entirely, that extraordinary moment when an angel came
to visit.

Secret Little Queen

She knew the God of her forefathers was always reaching into ordinary moments, into the lives of ordinary men and women, and drawing forth his miraculous plans. She knew the sacred verses that told
of Abraham and Sarah, of Moses and the Israelites, of Queen Esther

and Mordecai. So many marvelous deeds happened among her people because the Lord always remembers his covenant.

So shall you put these, my words, on your heart and on your soul—went the Shema—*and you shall bind them for signs on your hands, and they shall be for frontlets between your eyes* . . .

But on that ordinary day of the angel, the unspoken question fell to her. Yahweh desired to become man, desired a human visage. And then there was the great pause, such astonishing freedom, when God waited—*he waited*—for her.

There was no question of denying the request, only a child's wondering at these two things keeping such company: a vow of virginity and motherhood. But God always has a way.

She would say it then, and again and again and again: *Be it done unto me.*

The angel reached out then and, with his own shining hands, placed it upon her little virgin-girl's head: her crown. It would be with her always, this secret joy. *A crown is for royalty*, she thought, her heart dancing. *How he lifts up the lowly!*

Although it was hidden from the eyes of the world—even her beloved Joseph only now and then caught a glimpse of it—she surely felt its weight. Ever-burning hot beneath the shimmering gold and brilliant jewels, there was another crown, too, a bitter twist of thorns. And here—she could sense it already, her child's heart fluttering, the piercing burden of vicious wood.

Your Majesty

My office is perched at the end of the hall on the third floor of a grand old home that has been repurposed. It's an odd little office with an angled ceiling and a funky floor plan that no one else was anxious to claim, but I chose it precisely because, situated two floors beneath it, is the altar and tabernacle of our small chapel. Mass and adoration are celebrated there during the week, and throughout my day I like to imagine all the holiness hovering beneath me, holding me up, the altar very literally beneath my desk. And I thank God for the extraordinary privilege—that a layperson should get to work where the Eucharist is in repose.

And, truly, what better metaphor than to begin my workday by essentially placing my whole person on the altar. God is generous.

This is where I also meet with women to talk about prayer and what God is up to in their lives. I think of it as a kind of holding court—not my court. Every woman who plops down into my cozy spiritual direction nook—the heartbroken, the weary, the wondering, the hopeful—every one of them is royalty, a queen in the making. Most do not know this. Most would laugh aloud at the suggestion. Most have had their royal lineage shamed right out of them, that "Who do you think you are?" of the world beaten into their bones. So sometimes, they shrink and shrivel into tiny caricatures of themselves. *I don't want to offend anyone.* They lose the ability to see their own nobility and dignity. They begin to believe the lie that there was never a crown there in the first place. They only dared to imagine long ago, when they were young and naïve, that they too had given their lives so completely. *I don't want to look foolish.*

Or maybe they're confused. Too many of us mistake "princess" for "queen." We think of privileges and power, not authority; we think of physical beauty and a luxurious wardrobe, not strength of character hard-won. We think of private jets flown to exotic isles, not flights into a foreign land in the dead of night, hunted and hated, you and your infant child. We think of the kind of wealth that brings complete autonomy; we never think of that bloody birthright that binds us to the utter poverty that is the foot of the Cross.

We often meditate on the coronation, Mary crowned queen of heaven and earth following her assumption, body and soul, into heaven, and so tradition tells us we should. Though I want to argue for something more, that her coronation began the moment she said yes to the great desire of Adonai. She entered fully into her divine inheritance the moment she consented to the Lord. The moment she said, "You have my permission to take my life and put it to your purposes in whatever way you choose; I trust you," through the power of God Almighty, she then became mother—and queen. And though she would never have articulated it in this way, she was given a kingdom to steward and rule, guard and guide, like every queen.

Her kingdom was the Christ child.

A woman leaves behind her days of princessing when she has cultivated the ability to receive the fullness of grace that heaven intends for her. Not a bit of grace, not a smidgeon, a *fullness* of grace. If we have told the Lord that he may have our lives and do with them as he will, if we have offered our daily *fiats* great and small, then we've been given a kingdom too, to guard and guide, to nourish and tend, to rule with wisdom and mercy. The first question we need to ask ourselves is this: who or what is my kingdom?

The second is: how is my kingdom doing?

Such a Time as This

Esther's kingdom was in peril. Oh, but she knew how to be queen!

You will remember the story. In brief, Esther was essentially an orphan, raised by her cousin Mordecai, a faithful Jew. When the call went out from King Ahasuerus to replace Queen Vashti, Esther was chosen for consideration. After a year of preparations, she was presented to the king. She was found to be pleasing above all others and was made queen. Mordecai advised her to be mum on the fact that she was a Jew. A bit of foresight on his part, but we'll get to that.

One of the first things she did as queen—through information obtained through her faithful cousin—was to expose an assassination plot, saving the king. This deed and Mordecai's involvement were written into the official record.

Later, when Haman, a vain, self-absorbed underling of the king, became angry that Mordecai would not bow to him, the real trouble began. Mordecai prayed earnestly before the Lord: "I did this so that I might not set human glory above the glory of God, and I will not bow down to anyone but you, who are my Lord. . . . O Lord, do not destroy the lips of those who praise you" (Esther 13:14, 17).

Still, a decree went out declaring the imminent genocide of the Jewish people—Esther's people. Through a few messages back and forth about this predicament, Mordecai exhorted Esther to try to save her people by approaching the king. He said, "Who knows? Perhaps you have come to royal dignity for just such a time as this" (4:14). Esther was moved by his entreaty and asked for help, that all would fast for three days on her behalf. She and her maids put on sackcloth and ashes and joined in the fast. She was resolved to approach the king—an unlawful act, did we mention?—and with great courage, upon penalty of death, she declared, "If I perish, I perish" (4:16).

She was stricken, we are told, with a "deadly anxiety." She begged the Lord, "Save me from my fear!" (14:19) but not before reminding him of his faithfulness and power: "Make yourself known in this time of our affliction and give me courage. . . . Put eloquent speech in my mouth before the lion" (14:13).

In an age when our culture is sold the notion of independence and self-sufficiency as ultimate enlightenment, it's important to point out the distinction Esther made. A queen does not create herself. She is first prepared and then appointed, often at a time undetermined by her. She is raised up, not by her own power but on the authority of another. The authority she wields is authority that is given, received. The queen's work is to discover, receive, steward, and tend her respective kingdoms. Esther recognized that her true power came from the

God of her forefathers. As queen and steward of her people, she must act on their behalf, and she broached the highest and most powerful court imaginable, the Lord God Almighty, to intercede for their lives.

Eventually, along with a few lavish banquets, Esther's beauty and honor convinced the king to hear her. Though she was "radiant with perfect beauty and looked calm as though beloved, her heart was frozen with fear." In this state, she dared to say, "How can I bear to see the calamity that is coming on my people? Or how can I bear to see the destruction of my kindred?" (7:6) The king was deeply moved with compassion for his queen and furthermore was reminded through the reading of the official record of Mordecai's allegiance. He ordered that Haman receive the precise death he had planned for Mordecai, Mordecai was given a position of honor and authority, and justice had its day—and all because a queen never forgets her people. And she never forgets from whence true and perfect power is issued.

Esther wasn't after power; she was quaking in her royal slippers. She wasn't after empowerment either but rather the protection of her kindred. Esther was not conjuring her empowered self. She didn't stand in front of the mirror reciting affirmations before approaching the king: "I am capable." Instead, she got low and fasted and prayed and reminded God how powerful he was, because she knew where real power, real authority lies. And she was willing to receive and properly wield the authority that had been given to her.

Worth noting: the feast of Purim, which commemorates this event in Jewish tradition, is not a celebration of Esther; it is a remembrance of the faithfulness of God in saving his people. Hidden in the fete, however, is an important lesson: Esther knew how to be queen—because she knew her King.

In the New Testament, spiritual queenship takes on no less importance but perhaps a subtler comportment. Let's pay close attention. We have to be careful not to simply dress up a hyperactive spirituality and call it empowerment on behalf of the women of the church. We don't pray for power; we pray for *grace.*

A Holy Little Nothing

In my office, there's a chair that has been lovingly nicknamed "the chair of weeping." I cannot tell you how often women end up sitting in that chair and doing just that, weeping. The women I am a companion to in prayer so often come in and collapse with exhaustion. They are running on empty, beyond empty. They have worked themselves into a kind of spiritual bankruptcy, and my chair is the last stop before oblivion.

It is too common an experience. If you have any inclination whatsoever toward service, especially service within the church, you know: the need is endless. The world is hard, people are suffering, and we're trying to be good Christian people in this hard, suffering, terrorized world. We try and try and give and give, and it takes a toll.

Some years ago, a Catholic missionary came to visit my classroom. She worked in rather dangerous areas of the developing world, helping to start schools and businesses that especially serve to educate women and children. She did this in a place where it's not necessarily safe or sanctioned to educate a girl. So, she's quite a brave thing.

She was speaking of her work abroad, and she told the class that she was very heartened to overhear one of the children ask another child, "What does 'Catholic' mean?" The word—"Catholic"—was in the title of her organization. Without a moment's hesitation, the other child responded, "'Catholic' means 'help.'"

"Catholic" means "help."

Catholic means the Little Sisters of the Poor and the Missionaries of Charity and every holy order out there—Franciscan, Cistercian, Jesuit, Benedictine. Catholic means a warm meal and a warm bed. Catholic means medical attention when no one else will treat you.

Catholic means you can be educated—perhaps by a Dominican—taught a skill when no one else thinks you're worth educating. Catholic means that at every Mass someone somewhere is praying for you. If you need help, someone Catholic somewhere in the world is holding you before the throne of heaven. Every holy Mass assures us of this. The daily office assures us of this. The efforts of the Magnificat and other such resources assure us of this. The lives and charisms of hermits and the cloistered assure us of this.

Just think how many masses are celebrated around the world every day and what this must mean to so many in need of help, so many who have no one to pray for them.

"Catholic" means "help." And aren't we glad that it does? Aren't we grateful that we have been raised up in a spiritual posture that encourages us to grow in generosity, to stretch this virtue, as St. Teresa of Kolkata used to say, "Until it hurts a little bit"?

But first things first. It is better to give than to receive—so goes the axiom—but unless you first receive, you have nothing to give. And the Blessed Mother embodied her "nothingness" with perfect holiness.

If the Annunciation is Mary's coronation, a bestowal, it is also a radical act of reception. To give well, to give generously and meaningfully, we must first receive well, and generously. We must order our lives in such a way that what we are receiving—through our eyes, through our ears, into our mouths, into our hearts and souls, in our prayer—what we are accepting into ourselves is good and nourishing to the soul. And Mary can help show us the way.

Luke's Gospel sets the stage:

> In the sixth month of Elizabeth's pregnancy, God sent the angel Gabriel to Nazareth, a town in Galilee, to a virgin pledged to be married to a man named Joseph, a descendant of David. The

virgin's name was Mary. The angel went to her and said, "Greetings, you who are highly favored! The Lord is with you."

Mary was greatly troubled at his words and wondered what kind of greeting this might be. But the angel said to her, "Do not be afraid, Mary; you have found favor with God. You will conceive and give birth to a son, and you are to call him Jesus. He will be great and will be called the Son of the Most High. The Lord God will give him the throne of his father David, and he will reign over Jacob's descendants forever; his kingdom will never end."

"How will this be," Mary asked the angel, "since I am a virgin?"

The angel answered, "The Holy Spirit will come on you, and the power of the Most High will overshadow you. So the holy one to be born will be called the Son of God. Even Elizabeth your relative is going to have a child in her old age, and she who was said to be unable to conceive is in her sixth month. For no word from God will ever fail."

"I am the Lord's servant," Mary answered. "May your word to me be fulfilled." Then the angel left her. (Luke 1:26–38, New Jerusalem Bible)

The Mariologist Fr. Paul Haffner makes a critically important point about this passage:

> The expressions "full of grace" and "you who enjoy God's favour" . . . convey the idea of a change of something in the person or thing affected . . . that of a change brought about by grace . . . What is essential here is the affirmation that Mary has been transformed by the grace of God . . . Mary is the *recipient* of the first fruits of the Redemption . . . The angel's invitation, "Mary, do not be afraid; you have won God's favour," is a reassurance that *God is acting*. It stresses that Mary is the *recipient of a unique favour* and privilege in the history of salvation.[68]

We don't want to miss this. *God is acting. Mary is receiving.* God is giving, Mary is receiving. God is taking the virginal emptiness of Mary and filling it with purpose and giving it a precise shape: the shape of the Savior. God is acting. Mary is receiving God's favor.

And what's more, so are you. You are a part of the history of salvation. You are to receive the favor of God. God desires to act in you.

Are you ready to receive? Is there room, even a well-prepared emptiness in you—to receive the grace of God? Are you in touch with your own holy nothingness?

Rich in Emptiness

Receptivity is a challenge because it invites us to confront our own need, our dependence, our unworthiness, and our frailties. As we've mentioned, the axiom suggests that it may be better to give than to receive, but it is not necessarily easier. There are probably a few reasons for this. As women, I think we are programmed to give; we find it natural, we enjoy it, and we're good at it. Receiving, however, touches on a vulnerability we are not keen to express. Maybe it has been abused, taken advantage of, mocked, or rejected. To receive assumes a need, a limitation, an emptiness—and we're Catholic! We're helpers. We help, we give, we're there for you. *I am supposed to be a giver, right? Until it hurts?*

But let's not reduce the fullness of the gift. Receiving grace is always rooted in the most profound humility, and in the spiritual economy, it might be true to suggest that the more pure and profound your humility, the greater and more powerful graces you are available to receive. Simon Tugwell writes of the notion developed by the early desert fathers: "If we lose humility, we lose everything . . . any tendency to forget that we owe all our achievements to God will simply result in the final madness, which is pride."[69]

Did you catch that? Pride is madness. That is, if we lose our neediness, if we refuse to receive, there's danger ahead. And perhaps not only madness but great, sweeping loneliness as well.

Saying "Be it done unto me" is not only an act of obedience, or assent, but of receptivity. Mary recognizes her lowliness and in perfect reference to it accepts what is given by God. God has done this, she says. It is God's work, and Mary has simply been willing to receive it.

Receptivity has gotten a bad rap over the past two millennia. Some of that can be traced all the way back to the ancient Greeks. When Aristotle and others were trying to create a vocabulary that would express the differences between the sexes, they were working without the benefit of genetics. Some of the terms they grappled with we know are wrong, clearly. For example, Aristotle thought of women as substantially imperfect; a girl was "a boy gone wrong." Looking literally at anatomy, some of the train of thought became this: Men were associated with being active and women with being receptive. Men were actors, women were acted upon—that is, helpless. That may not have been the intention or the belief of the Greeks in its entirety, but we live in a fallen world, and there are bound to be errors. Receptivity was sometimes understood as a liability and a weakness. Extend that thought to women in a culture that encourages them to take "assertiveness training" and you can see how we got into a terrible mess.

We still don't like to think of women as receptive because we think it means that women cannot initiate (tell that to Mother Teresa), or that women cannot lead (tell that to Joan of Arc or Catherine of Siena), or that it's a sign of weakness to be in the position of receiving (tell that to Teresa of Ávila or any of the mystics). Receptivity is crucial for any revelation.

But receptivity in the church, and as a particularly feminine trait, has been rewritten, rediscovered, and renewed as a great and necessary strength, and the church had a fair amount to do with that "renovation."

We can mark a significant contribution in *Mulieris Dignitatem* by John Paul when he writes: "The moral and spiritual strength of a woman is joined to her awareness that God entrusts the human being to her in a special way." This was such a remarkable claim that in 2013, a seminar was held at the Vatican about it. Scholars from around the world came to discuss just what this means. In the very first presentation on this topic—the entrustment of the human person to women—the dean from the John Paul II Institute for Studies on Marriage and Family in Rome, Fr. Livio Melina, opened with this comment: "'Woman, here is your son.' These words that Jesus spoke as he was dying on the cross, words addressed to his mother entrusting her with the beloved disciple John, included with John all of the emerging Church. This is certainly the scene that inspired the great anthropological insight that John Paul placed at the center [of this apostolic letter]."[70]

John Paul invites a fresh view. "He does not interpret receptivity as a liability," writes Livio, "but rather as a key activity . . . necessary for a full understanding of love insofar as receiving is an indispensable prerequisite for created beings to be able to give themselves. Feminine receptivity therefore expresses a characteristic of created beings before their Creator."[71] In the manner of John Paul, receptivity, and in particular feminine receptivity, is the highest expression of cooperation with God. And it is always expanding, being refined, reborn.

At the Annunciation, Mary received her Christ-child kingdom. At the foot of the Cross, she received a remarkable expansion to her territory: all the young Christian church. A queen's territory often changes, expands.

When women come into my office and collapse and pour themselves out, empty themselves, they sometimes seem surprised and are often relieved to discover that I am encouraged by that. Good! I say. Get good and empty! Mary's first gift to us, her first act in the Annunciation, was to receive, and you cannot receive if there's no space, no empty corner. Yes, she brought Jesus to us; she brings us to Jesus and Jesus to us in every moment of her life. And we are called to do exactly the same: to bring Jesus to others. But here, the first thing she did was to listen and receive. Her first gift was not giving, but receiving, receiving grace and favor from God and not just a little grace, a smidgeon of grace, but a *fullness of grace,* and there had to be space inside her to do it. A holy, virginal emptiness.

The Hollow in the Cup

There are different kinds of emptiness, and I want to be very clear about what I mean. Note the distinction Caryll Houselander makes:

> Emptiness is a very common complaint in our days, not the purposeful emptiness of the virginal heart and mind but a void, meaningless, unhappy condition. Strangely enough, those who complain the loudest of the emptiness of their lives are usually people whose lives are overcrowded, filled with trivial details, plans, desires, ambitions, unsatisfied cravings for passing pleasures, doubts, anxieties and fears. . . . They dread space, for they want material things crowded together, so that there will always be something to lean on for support.[72]

But in the same way that John Paul invites a fuller view of receptivity, Houselander invites us to redefine emptiness, to reorder it. This holy virginal emptiness, she says,

> is not a formless emptiness, a void without meaning; on the contrary it has a shape, a form given to it by the purpose for which it is intended. It is emptiness like the hollow in the reed . . . to receive the piper's breath and to utter the song that is in the heart.

It is emptiness like the hollow in the cup, shaped to receive water or wine. It is emptiness like that of the bird's nest, built in a round warm ring to receive the little bird.[73]

Each of us possesses some manner of virginal emptiness as the Blessed Mother did, just waiting for the Lord to fill it with his grace. If you don't know what yours is, you can ask him. Take the question to Jesus. Houselander asks it this way:

In what way are we to fulfil the work of giving Christ life in us? Are we reed pipes? Is He waiting to live lyrically through us? Are we chalices? Does He ask to be sacrificed in us? Are we nests? Does He desire of us a warm, sweet abiding in domestic life at home? These are only some of the possible forms of virginity; each person may find some quite different form, his own secret.[74]

Because Mary's emptiness, her receptivity, was so perfect, Mary's own secret was the form, the physical man-God person of the Savior. And that act of receptivity was magnified further still at the foot of the Cross when she received John. And in that moment, a sweeping, cosmic kind of motherhood was given to her over all the church.

What is your own secret form? What form of Jesus are you being asked to carry into the world? Perhaps like Mary at the foot of the Cross, your earthly mothering is mostly finished; where might the Lord like to send you next? What might he like to give you next? How is your kingdom expanding?

Mary knew that she had been given something, had received something magnificent. She ran to tell her best girlfriend: "My soul magnifies the Lord. . . . for the Mighty One *has done* great things for me." He did the doing! Mary thought of nothing but God's providence. I think she must have been heroically *empty*, empty like the chalice awaiting the Precious Blood. We needn't run from or fear feelings of emptiness. Emptiness of this kind indicates a heroic readiness to serve God; emptiness can indicate extraordinary spiritual poise; emptiness can mean that you're finally ready for God to come and really do some incredible work with you. That you are ready—not to give—but first to receive. First to recognize your absolute dependence on God's grace. First to embrace the humility of this position. First to say thank you, I know I cannot accomplish any good work on my own, thank you for the grace to do all that you ask.

We simply ask: How is it that you wish me to bring Jesus to the world? What obstacles might be keeping me from emptying myself for you?

No word of God will ever fail. You are an important part of the history of salvation. All things are possible if we, like Mary, are willing to first receive all that God wishes to give, withholding no portion of ourselves from being filled by his light and his love. God can do great things with the empty, weeping women in my office. All the might and glory of salvation chose to pour himself into a little holy nothingness.

The Final Falling

Drifting into sleep, her last sleep, her eyes closed on this world and opened on another. Once again, instead of darkness, there was light, such light, glorious, pure, so inviting, *everywhere*. And one last time she would let it swallow her whole in a sweet and sweeping communion. The evening prayers she knew so well, the litany of God's faithfulness, were still beating in her breast.

Keep these words that I am commanding you today in your heart. Recite them to your children and talk about them when you are at home and when you are away, when you lie down and when you rise (Deuteronomy 6:6–7). . . . And up and up she rose with all the angels singing, "Arise, shine, for your light has come and the glory of the Lord has risen upon you." Their words filled the air with a sweet aroma.

Then came the faces.

A myriad to greet her: Joseph was first and he radiated joy. Anna and Joachim were with him, and Simeon. So many to see and to meet. She saw the women coming next, Esther and Judith, Sarah and Susannah, a glistening sea of others. And beyond them, oh, just beyond, they beckoned her forward and to the most beautiful face of all, the beaming countenance of her Son. He approached her with such tenderness it caught her up for a moment. But before they could even embrace, he bent low and reverently and kissed her feet and anointed them. Those feet that had carried her again and again into the temple. Those feet that had carried her to cousin Elizabeth—"Great things he has done for me!" Those feet that fled into Egypt in the dead of night, and danced at the wedding at Cana. Those feet that would not be moved from the foot of the Cross and took the steps to the upper room. These that now crush the head of the serpent.

As Jesus arose, angels appeared carrying a royal garment. It was of such breathtaking beauty that as he placed it upon her, she nearly gave way. But when it rested on her shoulders, it seemed familiar somehow, though she had certainly never owned anything so fine. It fit perfectly and filled her with a strange new sense of vitality and relief at the same time.

Then Jesus stretched out his hand and, gently touching her forehead, her crown—the crown that had been with her all those long years, that crown that bore deep within its dark and terrible reaches those bitter thorns, that crown that sometimes very nearly pinned her down with its pitiless weight—was brought to perfection in an instant. It was unveiled and revealed before all of heaven. And all of heaven was astounded by its radiance.

Jesus slid behind her then. He lifted her arms out wide and clasped her hands and they stood there together, arms raised, like Moses with Hur and Aaron beside him holding up his arms during the battle.

Opening before her was all of creation, heaven and earth, and pulsing through it all, living and eternal, was every single soul.

"Behold, Mother," Jesus said, "it pleases the Father to give you the kingdom."

It was then she noticed her cloak was *alive*. Yes, she had brought with her every prayer, every longing, every wound and want—a universe of need had been stitched into her heavenly raiment with one single, unending, golden thread. And she would never remove it. A queen never abandons her people.

With her shimmering crown and luminous, living mantle, she bowed before the Christ and joined in the song all around her: *Holy, Holy, Holy is the Lamb.*

Fr. Vann reminds us:

> You have in Mary, the Mother of mercy, the figure of what you have to be. It may be particular men—husband, children, friends—who will come to you so; it may be your vocation to share with Mary something of her universal pity, but to renew the soil of the world only indirectly, through your own inner experience and unexpressed pity. But somehow, in some way, you must share her vocation, you must share the glory of the destiny of which she is the symbol and the supreme expression; for only so can you share as you should in the restoring of the world, and only so will you yourself be made whole.[75]

You know it's true. We must share in the glory of her royal destiny.

Sisters, our kingdoms are under siege. Time to release the queen. Time to call forth her courts, to put on sackcloth and ashes, to fast and intercede as she never has before. It's time to approach the kings of the world. If we perish, we perish. The Lord will put eloquent speech in our mouths before the lion.

Christ Encounter

Pray: As you settle into prayer, ask the Holy Spirit to guide your prayer and meditation.

Through the intercession of Mary, Queen of Heaven and Earth, pray with Luke 1:26–38. Ask the Lord to show you how you might share in the queenship of Mary.

Suggestions for meditation:

- Where are you in the scene?
- What strikes you most about this exchange between Gabriel and Mary? Is there a word or phrase that sticks out? What does it mean to you?
- Do you remember a particular fiat in your own life, a moment you said yes to the will of the Father? What did that feel like? What were the results of that yes?
- Is there a current fiat before you, an invitation to serve and to build up the kingdom in some new way?
- How is the Lord asking you to guard and guide his kingdom?
- Converse with him about this.

Write: What movements of heart took place in your prayer? How did you feel at the start and then at the end of your prayer?

Doxology: Give thanks for the prayer you have just experienced.

Questions for Small-Group Discussion

- What does Kelly mean when she writes of "emptiness" as a grace?
- In what ways is God calling you to share in Mary's vocation to restore the world? How do you know?

CLOSING: DISCIPLE

"Come and see a man who told me everything."
—John 4:29

It was her father who first introduced her to the sea. Business would sometimes take him all the way to the coast of the Great Sea, and on one special trip, she accompanied him.

Her young eyes had never imagined anything so big; the water seemed to stretch out forever. She could still remember the smell and the sounds, the sand and the rocks, so many birds, the surprising salty taste that wrinkled her nose when she tasted a drop. Her father laughed and crouched down with her on the shore, and scooping up the warm white sand, he poured it into her tiny hands. "Catch it," he said, smiling. "Catch it, now."

She cupped her hands tightly, but still the sand fell away through her fingers bit by bit. As she struggled to contain it, to her surprise and delight, a glistening little seashell was slowly revealed. She turned to her father, holding out her palm, and said, "Look, Papa! See what I found!"

"Yes, child," he smiled. "A little treasure to take with you from our journey together."

From that moment, her heart was set on the shell. She would carry it back to their tent with all the focus and care she could. She would study it from every angle, the soft pink grooves, the smooth slope of the underside, the scalloped edge. And that night, she placed the seashell on a pillow propped beside her and fell asleep listening to the voice of her father, as he told her the story of the shell's life and how it had come to find her and make its home with her.

She often woke up dreaming of the sea, the fresh air, the voice of Papa. It all felt very far away now. *Had it even happened, that trip to the shore?* She opened her eyes on the morning, and the dream vanished like a thin mist.

She took a deep breath and sighed. *No time for wondering now.* She steeled herself against the coming day. There was much to do.

Except for her father, men, in her experience, were not easily pleased. She had known too many of them. Not long after her father died, there was the first marriage—then divorce, scandal, shame. On and on it went, so many desperate choices, so much hope wasted, again and again, discarded like so much rubbish. The constant strain to simply survive. She felt shriveled inside, like a dried leaf waiting to be crushed underfoot.

The man under whose roof she currently resided was no exception. She would need to work hard if she wanted to keep from starving on the streets.

Her mornings were spent cooking what she could, mending, feeding the animals. She didn't mind that work and even enjoyed the animals. They were always happy to see her with the hay in her hands. They harbored no ill judgment toward her.

The hardest chore—the one she dreaded—was fetching the water.

Water. Always they needed more of it. Hoisting those terrible, heavy pots. It was the worst part of her day. She would go, as she always did, when the sun was highest in the sky. The brutal heat would keep most everyone else away. She could avoid their vicious tongues then. Even gossips couldn't take the noonday heat. So when the sun burned brightest, she made her way to the well. She slipped through the markets. She knew the least crowded streets. It took longer this way, but at least she could stay out of sight.

When she reached the open place where the well stood, she scanned the area from the protection of a bush. Satisfied that she could proceed without notice, she put her head down, lowered her eyes, and approached. She put her pot down in the dirt and leaned over the edge of the well to look at the brooding, stagnant pool below. It was the well of her forefathers. How long had her ancestors been coming to this place, drawing up from the deepest recesses all that would sustain them? Again, her heart longed for the sea, something fresh, anything clean and new.

Then she heard a voice behind her. "Woman, give me a drink."

She turned to see a man, a Jew, sitting in the shade.

This must be a trick, she thought, looking around for one of the gossip mongers to pop out from behind a tree. *No Jewish man would ever approach a Samaritan, a woman. No one would ever approach me.* Her heart filled with dread. The last thing she needed was more scandal.

But there was no one to jeer, just the man there with her. Still, she hesitated to reply. Long experience had taught her that men were not to be trusted in even the simplest matter. But this one had a kind face, and he looked sincerely thirsty. There was something else, too. He looked her in the eye, looked at her in a way she had not been looked at in a long, long while—as one person looks at another person. She caught herself looking back at him, and when their eyes met, she immediately dropped her glance.

"Sir, Jews have no dealings with Samaritans," she said, looking at her dusty feet. "How is it that you ask me, a woman, for a drink?"

The man sat up a bit then, so she took a step back. Perhaps she had offended him, said too much.

But there was no offense in his tone. He spoke slowly, deliberately, directly to her: "If you knew the gift of God, and who it is that is saying to you 'Give me a drink,' you would have asked him and he would have given you living water."

She looked up at him once again. He had no bucket. Maybe the brutal heat of the day left the poor man confused. "Sir, you have nothing to draw with, and the well is deep; where do you get that living water?"

"Everyone who drinks of this water will thirst again, but whoever drinks of the water that I shall give him will never thirst." The man continued to look at her intensely. "The water that I shall give him will become in him a spring of water welling up to eternal life."

His words were strange, but his voice was inviting. What well was this he described? She'd never heard of it. Could it be possible that she would never have to endure this unsavory task again? She almost grew hopeful.

"Sir, give me this water, that I may not thirst, nor come here to draw."

The man replied, "Go, call your husband and come here."

Her heart dropped. *I will never escape this life*, she thought. *I will be haunted the rest of my days. There will be no eternal life for me, only this living death. There is nowhere I might go and be free of this shame.*

"I have no husband," she said looking back at the ground as she prayed to die on the spot.

"You are right," said the man, "for you have had five husbands and he who you now have is not your husband."

She looked up, and the man met her with a penetrating gaze. As the man continued to speak, her thoughts raced through her life, from that moment of falling asleep with her shell, to losing her father, through every choice, through every miserable consequence, each time shamed out into the street. It was as if this stranger knew her, as if he were there in her mind too. He continued to speak, but she read other words in his eyes: *I know you, daughter. I know all you have done and all that has been done to you. I know this devastation. There is a way out.* I am *the way.*

He kept on. "The hour is coming and now is . . ."

This was not some simple passerby. He spoke of her worship, but what could he know of it? And what was this "spirit and truth"?

"I know the Messiah is coming," she said. "My father told me he will show us all things."

The man stood up slowly and said, "I who speak to you am he."

Suddenly she remembered the story her father told her so long ago, when she was just a child and had found that perfect seashell. He had filled her hands with sand, and that night, as she drifted into sleep, he told her how God arranges the world, right down to this seashell, that he gave it to her, and for her did he create it. He told her too of a Messiah, a great king who would come. He would come, and there would be light and rescue.

Her father had always known. Had always had a deep confidence in the master of the universe. He told her that he felt the master's presence in the sea and the wind and the sunrise, in the fields of wheat, and walking under the olive trees. "And I can see his goodness in you, my daughter."

She wanted to fall at the man's feet, to beg his name, but a small group of men approached, so she stood still. They were murmuring among themselves, she could hear it: "Is he talking with a woman? What could he be doing?"

The man surely heard them too, but he kept his gaze on her. And in that gaze, she knew that she was *known*. It was as if she were the only person alive to him.

When the others drew near, she could not bear to be still a second longer. With a final glance at the man, she left her water jar and hurried away. She found herself running all the way into the heart of the city, into the midst of those who took such joy in her demise. But she didn't care, because everything her father had told her was true. There was rescue and light and a way, and she had looked upon *his* face.

"Come!" she called out. "Come and see a man who told me everything I have ever done."

Whom does Jesus call? Whom does he invite to become his disciple? What are the criteria? Are there criteria unique to women?

When I was in Rome years ago, I had the chance to meet and speak with the wonderful German philosopher, mother, wife, and grandmother Hanna-Barbara Gerl-Falkovitz. Her work is especially well known in Europe, and this tiny mite of a woman nearly knocked me down with her erudition on Christ's interactions with women. She wrote an excellent article about some of the radical countercultural changes manifested by the Lord, and in it she offers a tidy and compelling list of just what Jesus launched when he entered the human history of womankind:

- Women traveled with Jesus; women sat at his feet, listening and learning and being challenged—there was an assumption that they were teachable and worth teaching.
- They were allowed to approach Jesus, even touch him, without penalty or rebuke.
- The traditional male authority structure was rewritten; service became a sign of one's authority, not power or dominance, and that meant women would be served too—by men, husbands, fathers, sons, brothers, and one another.
- Jesus was as concerned with the conversion—*metanoia*—of women as he was the metanoia of men.

- In all his interactions with women and in all his teaching, he raised women from the rank of possession to being their own person.

- Remarkably, he knew women by their names. He knew their stories, their deepest inner realities and aches, their fears and failures, their hopes and desires; *he knew them by heart.* This knowledge was not held over their heads as a means of manipulation or control but rather was offered in a merciful, liberating, affirming, and dignifying way.

The Samaritan woman at the well stands out in a unique way because she experienced the fullness of this arc of merciful liberation in only moments—something most of us move through in a lifetime. She was moved in part by the countercultural Christ. He was engaging the least likely imaginable: poor, outcast, sinner, woman, Samaritan. He allowed the least likely to come close and look him in the eye. He treated her like a person, someone worth his notice and attention. But even more important, he regarded her as someone who deserved to hear the truth—about who he was *and* who she was. He revealed himself, and he revealed her too, telling her the full truth of her life. Mercy is always this two-way street, meeting Jesus and meeting ourselves in relationship to him.

Gerl-Falkovitz's final point is perhaps the most compelling. "It is clearly stated in the book of Leviticus that a woman's testimony is of less validity. However, it was women who were the main witnesses of the death and burial of Jesus, and they alone were the first witnesses of the resurrection."[76]

And so we return to the beginning and our sister Magdalene. We asked, whom does Jesus call? Whom does he invite to become his disciple? What are the criteria? Are there criteria unique to women?

Perhaps the better question for our final meditation is "How do I witness Jesus?"

Each of us has her own version of the Samaritan woman's hidden walk to the well, some part of our soul's story we want to keep hidden, something we want to escape or forget. Maybe we're ashamed or afraid; maybe we're angry, caught in stubbornness. But it is precisely here that Jesus comes to know us and to make us disciples. He brings us into the light to make us his witnesses. There's relief in standing in the full light of Christ because his judgment is perfect, his knowledge is total, his love is built on truth. We can trust that when Jesus tells us the truth, it is always a life-giving act of mercy.

Let's never lose sight of this monumental fact: when Jesus entered human history, he came to be a specific friend to a specific woman—and it's *you*. Jesus has accomplished all to honor your true heart, your lovely womanish soul. *He knows you by name; he knows you by heart.*

Go, and be his fearless, living woman witness.

ENDNOTES

1. Madeleine L'Engle, *Walking on Water: Reflections on Faith and Art* (Wheaton, IL: Shaw Publishers, 1980), 74.

2. Ibid. Emphasis added.

3. Ibid., 75.

4. Gerald Vann, OP, *The Divine Pity: A Study in the Social Implications of the Beatitudes* (New York: Sheed & Ward, 1946), 19.

5. Ibid., 20. Emphasis added.

6. Romano Guardini, *The Inner Life of Jesus: Pattern of All Holiness* (1957; Manchester, NH: Sophia Institute Press, 1992), 111, italics in the original.

7. *Mulieris Dignitatem*, § 19.

8. Psalm 28:2. All scriptural references are taken from the New Revised Standard Version unless otherwise noted.

9. Luke 8:42–48.

10. Hans Urs von Balthasar, *The Christian and Anxiety* (San Francisco: Ignatius Press, 2000), 81.

11. Ibid., 67.

12. John Wickham, SJ, *The Real Presence of the Future Kingdom* (Montreal: Ignatian Centre Publications, 1990), 74.

13. Fr. Richard McAlear, OMI, *The Power of Healing Prayer: Overcoming Emotional and Psychological Blocks* (Huntington, IN: Our Sunday Visitor, 2012), 73–74.

14. Ibid., 74.

15. Ibid., 14.

16. Hans Urs von Balthasar, *The Christian State of Life*, trans. Sr. Mary Frances McCarthy (San Francisco: Ignatius Press, 1983), 407.

17. *Guadiem et Spes* affirms that "man, who is the only creature on earth which God willed for itself, cannot fully find himself except through a sincere gift of himself" (24).

18. Caryll Houselander, *Essential Writings*, ed. Wendy M. Wright (Maryknoll, NY: Orbis Books, 2005), 131.

19. *Catechism of the Catholic Church* (Vatican City: Libreria Editrice Vaticana, 1994), 900.

20. Pope St. John Paul II, *Post-Synodal Apostolic Exhortation, Christifideles Laici* (Vatican City: Libreria Editrice Vaticana, 1988), 59.

21. Luci Swindoll, *Wide My World, Narrow My Bed: Living and Loving the Single Life* (New York: Multnomah Press, 1982).

22. Houselander, *Essential Writings*, 126.

23. Ibid., 147.

24. See Wright's commentary in *Essential Writings*, 33.

25. Ibid.

26. Ibid., 79.

27. Ibid., 34.

28. Ibid., 37.

29. Susan Annette Muto, *Celebrating the Single Life: A Spirituality for Single Persons in Today's World* (New York: Crossword Publishing, 1982), 144.

30. See Wright's commentary in Houselander, *Essential Writings*, 157.

31. *Essential Writings*, 166.

32. Ibid., 93.

33. Muto, *Celebrating the Single Life*, 84.

34. Ibid., 94.

35. Yves Congar, *Lay People in the Church: A Study for a Theology of the Laity* (Christian Classics, Revised Edition, 985), 432.

36. Ibid., 401.

37. Houselander's life further speaks to older single adults in the church in a unique way. She was forty years old before her first widely circulated work, *This War Is the Passion*, was published. In this respect, her life is reminiscent of St. Teresa of Calcutta, who did not begin her magnum opus, the Missionaries of Charity, until she was forty years old.

38. Jordon Aumann, OP, *Spiritual Theology* (London: Sheed & Ward, 1980), 33.

39. *Essential Writings*, 31.

40. Ibid., 110.

41. Ibid., 88.

42. Hans Urs von Balthasar, *The Christian State of Life*, 486.

43. I first heard this story in person from Fr. Paul Murray, who has the note. He later recorded it in his lovely book *I Loved Jesus in the Night—Teresa of Calcutta: A Secret Revealed* (Brewster, MA: Paraclete Press, 2008).

44. Ibid., 49–50.

45. *Christian State of Life*, 48.

46. Psalm 86:11.

47. Anne Marie Kidder, *Women, Celibacy, and the Church: Toward a Theology of the Single Life* (New York: Crossroad Publishing, 2003), 12.

48. John of the Cross, "Stanzas Applied Spiritually to Christ and the Soul," trans. Kieran Kavanaugh, OCD, and Otilio Rodriquez, OCD (San Francisco: Ignatius Press), 57–58.

49. A. G. Sertillanges, *What Jesus Saw from the Cross* (Manchester, NH: Sophia Institute Press, 1996), 133.

50. St. John Paul II, *Mulieris Dignitatem*, § 19.

51. Romano Guardini, *The Art of Praying* (New York: Pantheon Books, 1957), 22–23.

52. Gerald Vann, OP, *The Divine Pity: A Study in the Social Implications of the Beatitudes* (New York: Sheed & Ward, 1946), 141.

53. Ibid., 139.

54. Douglas Van Steere, *Gleanings: A Random Harvest*, "On Listening to Another" (New York: Harper Books, 1955).

55. Vann, *The Divine Pity*, 144.

56. Pope St. John Paul II, *Laborem Exorcens*, § 25. Emphasis added.

57. Ibid., § 26.

58. Romano Guardini, *The Art of Praying* (New York: Pantheon Books, 1957), 14.

59. Susan Cain, *Quiet: The Power of Introverts in a World That Can't Stop Talking* (New York: Crown Publishers, 2012).

60. Sherry Turkle, *Alone Together: Why We Expect More from Technology and Less from Each Other*, (New York: Basic Books, 2011), 166.

61. Guardini, *Inner Life of Jesus,* 15.

62. Ibid., 13.

63. Ibid., 34.

64. Edith Stein, *Essays on Woman*, 2nd rev. ed. (Washington, DC: ICS Publications, 1996), 56.

65. Ibid., 124.

66. Thomas Merton, *Faith and Violence: Christian Teaching and Christian Practice* (University of Notre Dame Press, 1968). Emphasis added.

67. As quoted by Robert J. Foster, *Prayer: Finding the Heart's True Home* (San Franscisco: Harper, 1992), 155.

68. Fr. Paul Haffner, *The Mystery of Mary* (Mundelein, IL: Hillenbrand Books, 2004), 56–58. Emphasis added.

69. Simon Tugwell, OP, *Ways of Imperfection* (Springfield, IL: Templegate Publishers, 1985), 32.

70. Fr. Livio Melina, "God Entrusts the Human Being to the Woman," Pontifical Council of the Laity (Vatican City: Libreria Editrice Vaticana, 2013), 21.

71. Ibid., 26.

72. Caryll Houselander, *Reed of God* (Notre Dame, IN: Ave Maria Press, 2006), 22.

73. Ibid., 21.

74. Ibid., 24.

75. Vann, *The Divine Pity,* 144.

76. Hanna-Barbara Gerl-Falkovitz, "Jesus of Nazareth, Mary, and the Women in the Gospel and in the Early Church," *Woman and Man: The Humanum in Its Entirety*, Pontifical Council for the Laity (Vatican City: Libreria Vaticana, 2010), 53.

ABOUT THE AUTHOR

Elizabeth (Liz) Kelly is an award-winning speaker and the author of six books, including *Reasons I Love Being Catholic*, which won the Catholic Press Association first-place award for Best Popular Presentation of the Faith in 2007. Her written works frequently appear in the *Magnificat* Lenten and Advent Companions and in other Catholic venues, such as the *Catholic Spirit*. Kelly received her certification as a spiritual director from the Cenacle of our Lady of Divine Providence School of Spirituality in association with the Franciscan University of Steubenville in 2015. She works with the Ignatian exercises and leads retreats with a particular focus on helping women flourish in their faith. Kelly has appeared on Public Radio, Boston Catholic Television, EWTN, and Salt and Light Television. She is presently the managing editor of *Logos: A Journal of Catholic Thought and Culture* at the University of St. Thomas (MN) and teaches in the Catholic Studies program. She is author of the nationally syndicated column "Your Heart, His Home." Her schedule, along with sample podcasts of her speaking, may be found on her website: https://www.lizk.org.